BORDERLAND THEOLOGY

By Jerry H. Gill

WIPF & STOCK · Eugene, Oregon

Wipf and Stock Publishers
199 W 8th Ave, Suite 3
Eugene, OR 97401

Borderland Theology
By Gill, Jerry H.
Copyright©2003 by Gill, Jerry H.
ISBN 13: 978-1-5326-9023-5
Publication date 5/1/2019
Previously published by The Ecumenical Program
on Central America and the Caribbean, 2003

Table of Contents

Preface v
Foreword vii

Introduction: Double Entendre 1

Part One: The Bible and the Borderlands

    Chapter One: The Incarnational Paradigm:
        The Word Became Flesh 9
    Chapter Two: The Hebrew Scriptures:
        Outsiders and Insiders 23
    Chapter Three: The Christian Scriptures:
        Insiders and Outsiders 39

Part Two: The Church and the Borderlands

    Chapter Four: The Church in World History:
        Conquering and Dividing 59
    Chapter Five: The Church in Chiapas, Mexico:
        The Ministry of Bishop Samuel Ruíz 75
    Chapter Six: The Church in a Mission of Reconciliation:
        Bridging Borders 93

Conclusion: The Search for Humane Borders 111

Appendices

Questions for Reflection 123
Resource Organizations 124
Migrant Deaths in 2000 126

Preface

by Jerry GIll

I believe that sound theological reflection must orbit around the interaction between the scriptures and one's own experience, and that is exactly how this book came into being. The experiential stimulus that I received from moving to the U.S.-Mexico border some nine years ago, and from connecting up with the BorderLinks organization, triggered my reflections on the role played by borders in both the Hebrew and Christian scriptures.

At first I was astounded by the fact that none of my college and graduate school education had ever touched on the role that borders and boundaries play in the biblical drama. Now it is clear to me that the dynamics surrounding the notion of borders may well be the most central and basic theme in both the Hebrew and Christian scriptures.

In a geo-political, cultural *and* theological sense, nearly all of the major events and concepts in the Bible involve some aspect of the notion of border crossing. The purpose of this book is to explain just how this is so by beginning with the notion of the Incarnation, of the Word becoming flesh, as a kind of cosmic border-crossing in which the Divine enters into human life in order to transform it.

In the development of this theme I have been greatly stimulated by the leadership of Rick-Ufford Chase and my other colleagues at BorderLinks. In the actual putting together of the manuscript I am immensely indebted to Kathy Ogle at EPICA. She repeatedly improved my overly abstract writing style by making it more concrete and to the point. Indeed, in places this is as much her work as it is mine. I am also, as always, deeply grateful for the encouragement and critiques offered by my wife and colleague Mari Sorri. She is almost always right!

Tucson, Arizona
May 20, 2003

Foreword

by Rick Ufford-Chase

I want to share a story of crossing borders.

Veronica is a single mother of a fourteen-year-old boy. She lives with her sister and brother-in-law in Mexico City. In July of 2002, she made a decision to leave her son with her family in order to go north with her nephew to look for work in the United States. Together, they traveled by bus to northern Sonora, just south of the Arizona border. In early August, they found a "coyote", a paid smuggler, to guide them through the Sonoran desert and across the U.S/Mexico border to Phoenix. From there, they planned to move further north to look for work in the interior of the United States.

The coyote transported them by van to the town of Sonoita, Sonora, right on the border and just south of the Tohono O'odham nation, a Native American reservation covering most of southwestern Arizona. They began hiking late in the afternoon, although temperatures would still have been well above one hundred degrees.

There were many potential dangers: an untrustworthy coyote who might rob or abandon them, dehydration or heat stroke that had already killed over a hundred others in that same area of the desert during the previous months, poisonous snakes and cactus that make the desert even more brutal with their own survival tactics in the desert. Finally, of course, there was the ever-present danger of being discovered by "la migra", the U.S. Border Patrol, and losing both their elusive hopes and all of the money they had invested in their journey.

After hiking all night and much of the next day, Veronica began to feel weak and nauseous. She was fighting a pounding headache, and could no longer keep up with the group. These were the classic first signs of heat stroke. The coyote insisted that she must keep up or she would be left behind, and he refused to slow the pace of the group. Her nephew stayed with her, but little by little the rest of the group began to pull away.

Eventually, Veronica collapsed. Her nephew waited until dusk when the desert was a little cooler, and then began to carry his aunt vaguely in the direction he believed would take him to the nearest highway. I have no idea how far he had to carry her, nor do I know exactly what happened when they reached the road. By the time I met Veronica ten days later, her nephew had moved on toward the north, and she couldn't remember any of the details. Someone must have found them however, because eventually they ended up in an emergency room of a Tucson Hospital.

I am told that Veronica was completely unconscious, and that her heart stopped beating twice as doctors tried to save her. She spent a full week in intensive care, and when I met her a few days later, her lips were still completely black, she couldn't speak, and she was being fed intravenously because her cerebral cortex had been damaged and she couldn't swallow.

Little by little over the coming week, she regained her ability to function. I was with her as she recovered her ability to speak, and as she took her first steps. Miraculously, twelve days after she survived her trauma she was again able to swallow and the doctor removed her feeding tube. It was unclear how much her brain had been affected by the trauma she had suffered, but it was very clear that her emotional capacity was intact as she wept through a telephone conversation with her son on his fourteenth birthday.

Finally, more than two weeks after her attempt to cross the border, the Mexican Consulate helped to purchase a plane ticket for her to return to Mexico City, and I took her to the airport to see her off. As she sat in a donated wheelchair waiting to board her flight, I asked her if it was worth it. "Knowing what you now know, would you recommend others try and cross the border without documents?"

Veronica was thoughtful about her answer. "In the end," she whispered, "I don't really feel like I have any way to provide my son with the future he deserves. There is no work that will pay me enough to keep him in school, and there is little chance that his life will be any better than my own."

Veronica is like hundreds of thousands of migrants and refugees in the world today who have been forced by war or disaster or their location on the underside of the global economy to cross borders in search of a better way of life. The Church, if it is going to be a meaningful institution in the world today, must come to terms with how it is going to understand and respond, theologically and practically, to the question of borders.

How will we define appropriate borders to protect individual cultures, particularly among indigenous peoples, as the world rushes toward a consumer monoculture and a single, global market that increasingly defines all of our communities? How will we name outsiders and insiders in a world and an economy where being "outside" or excluded is the functional equivalent of a life without hope, or even death, and where eighty percent of the world's population will not be invited to the table? How will we welcome the strangers in our midst once they have been forced into the role of nomad or migrant, become global wanderers without resources or options in their search for survival?

Finally, how will we seek full inclusion in the global community for everyone, especially those who have resisted the pressures to migrate but who find that they are functionally excluded from the global economy right there in their own communities?

This book is an important attempt to lay the Biblical, theological and historical groundwork to help us to answer those questions. After reading this book, it is evident to me - as it I believe it will be evident to you - that there is a strong theme about what happens to insiders and outsiders that runs throughout the Bible. The Bible is story after story of migrants who were forced to cross borders and the way they were received when they did. It is about politics and economics of exclusion that forced people to make the hard choices to leave to become migrants and cross borders.

But the Bible is also about the insiders who were risk-takers, and who dared to cross borders in order to redefine community and to seek full inclusion for everyone in the family of God. Theologically, in the end the Bible is a story of what Jerry calls the "incarnational paradigm," in which he sees a God prepared to become human in order to be fully present with God's people.

The borderlands between the United States and Mexico, where Jerry has chosen to make his home and develop a new sense of vocation over the last ten years, is a crucible in which the heat of one of the most important borders in the world forges new relationships, new ideas, and a new theology for those who dare to take it seriously. The work of building those relationships, engaging those ideas, and mapping a new theology is a risky enterprise. It is risky because crossing borders has always been considered subversive. That is certainly true in this place where migrants who are trying to survive have always been seen as a threat. They are seen as potential terrorists at worst, and as those who would steal first world jobs at best.

It is risky because welcoming the stranger has always been a radical act of daring. That's certainly been true for the last twenty years as people of faith in the borderlands have defied their governments to welcome political and economic migrants and try to protect their lives as they cross the border without documents.

Re-reading the Bible with an eye for borders and how God would have us respond insiders is not likely to be a popular exercise among a people who, by and large, are the beneficiaries of those borders. In the end, though, Jerry Gill has captured a very important idea. Crossing borders is about living our faith. If we can manage to cross a few borders in our lives, or to welcome others who have done so into our lives, perhaps we'll be able to re-imagine who God would like us to be. Put another way, it means acting into a new way to be Christian.

As you read this book, I invite you to think about the borders that surround and protect you in ways that are seen and unseen. What would it mean to your faith to question those borders? Who do you identify with in Jerry's stories from the Bible, or the early church, or the borderlands communities of today? In my experience, there is no more important set of questions that confront us a people of faith in our world today.

Welcome to the borderlands.

June 30, 2003

for

Wilys Claire and Jim Nelson

who know and care about such things

Introduction

Double *Entendre*

When we first came to live in Tucson, Arizona in 1994, I had never given any real thought to the role borders play in the world in general, let alone to their significance here at the place where Mexico and the United States meet. At that point, I knew nothing of the realities of life on the border. I was only vaguely aware of the pros and cons of the recently enacted North American Free Trade Agreement (NAFTA) policies and was sympathetically aware of the involvement of local churches in the 1980s in providing Sanctuary for political refugees from Central America.

After our arrival, however, my wife Mari Sorri and I became active members of Southside Presbyterian Church, which played a central role in the Sanctuary movement. In addition, we began to work in various capacities with an experiential educational enterprise called BorderLinks that seeks to facilitate understanding of border issues. Through this involvement I not only have come to a greater appreciation for and understanding of border politics and economics, but I have come to the conclusion that the concept of borders is at the heart of our political, economic and even spiritual lives as human beings on this planet.

Borders divide and separate people, assigning—usually—a more privileged space on one side and a less privileged space on the other. Throughout human history, as far back as the Old Testament stories that begin to define our Judeo-Christian religions, people have drawn lines in the sand to tell others, "You can come this far, no farther." Sometimes the lines are drawn by the weak in an attempt to protect themselves, but more often they are defined by the strong in order to guarantee themselves a greater measure of resources and power.

There is a straightforward sense in which the double meaning of the term "Borderland Theology" stands at the heart of what this book is about. On the one hand, it is concerned with literal, political borders that have existed throughout Judeo-Christian history and the serious difficulties they have generated for people on both sides of them. At the same time, this book is also about the symbolic social and spiritual borders that have arisen between and among the various peoples of the world. Thus the term "borderland" is to be taken in two senses simultaneously. It may apply to a concrete national border like the one that divides the United States from Mexico, for instance, or to social boundaries such as racism, sexism, or classism.

My purpose in these pages is to focus on the idea of borders both concretely and theologically. My thesis is that the notion of borders is crucial to a sound understanding of today's world and of God's activity in it. More specifically, I argue that the God of the Old and New Testament has consistently challenged people of faith to examine borders in light of God's all-inclusive vision of justice and to work to cross or dissolve any boundaries that exclude or oppress others.

For the most part, this book is written for Christians in the United States, though its ideas may be applied in many places. As a Christian, I am concerned with exploring the idea of the Incarnation as the fulcrum for more fully understanding the concept of borders and of God's perspective on them. Put bluntly, I am proposing that the Incarnation, in which the Divine Word is said to have directly entered into human life, should serve as the starting point for any analysis of the role borders play in our world today. For the Incarnation of Christ clearly embodies a paradigm case of "border crossing" in which God chose to step across the line or boundary that traditionally has been thought to separate divine and human life.

This way of putting things calls for some redefining of the key terms "border" and "Incarnation," for they are not generally spoken of in the same context. Nevertheless it is easy to see upon a little reflection that these two notions can be thought of as integrally interrelated because the central idea of the Incarnational claim is that the character of Divine reality refuses to be confined within human limits or boundaries, whether conceptual or socio-political. To "incarnate" Spirit into flesh is to cross from one side of a traditional division to the other.

The idea of double *entendre* is significant here as well. For, the very notion of Incarnation is itself a form of double *entendre* in that it affirms both the divinity and the humanity of the person of Jesus

Christ. In a word, Jesus "means" two different things at the same time; he signifies the transcendent and the human as integrated into one reality. As Paul put it: "God was in Christ reconciling the world to the Divine." In his life and ministry, Christ sought not only to break down the barriers between God and humanity, but also the ones built up between various groups of human beings.

In Chapter One of this book, I further develop this idea of the Incarnation as a border crossing and begin to explore the ways in which Jesus began to cross other boundaries in his ministry here on earth. Ultimately, my point is that this understanding of the meaning of the Incarnation can be fruitfully and directly applied to those aspects of border reality that divide and oppress people today. I believe U.S. Christians can learn a great deal from those who would cross our borders. We may also be called to become figurative border-crossers ourselves. The Incarnation and the life of Christ suggest ways of overcoming the negative ramifications and oppression so endemic to border situations and moving toward reconciliation and healing.

Chapters Two and Three look directly at the scriptures in order to show the centrality of the concept of borders and border-crossings in the Hebrew and Christian Scriptures. In the Hebrew Scriptures we see the wandering people of God crossing boundaries to search for a home. These our religious ancestors were not usually the conquerors or "winners" of their time. They were exiled, enslaved and mistreated. They were often the poor, the homeless, and the outcast. But there were also times when the Hebrew people invaded other nations and became oppressors, and there were times when they acted unjustly with each other. The important point is that God crossed borders with them, consistently calling for justice and giving special accompaniment to the outsiders of any given situation.

Likewise, in the New Testament from the Incarnation itself to the myriad of ways in which Jesus reaches out to the outcasts of his day, the commandment to cross boundaries to reconcile and to heal becomes abundantly clear. In Chapters Two and Three, I also refer to the concept of "insiders" and "outsiders," the two groups of people inevitably created by exclusionary borders.

In Chapter Four I look at the history of the Christian Church and come to the sad conclusion that our Church has failed in opportunity after opportunity to follow Christ's reconciling example. Instead, the Christian Church, like other institutions, has more frequently erected boundaries that separate insiders from outsiders, the privileged from the despised or oppressed.

There is good news, however, in Chapters Five and Six where I present two significant examples of faithful Christian border-crossing witness. The first is the life and work of Bishop Samuel Ruíz of Chiapas, Mexico and the second is the unique mission carried out by the organization BorderLinks, which I have been privileged to be a part of here in Tucson. These examples help us to visualize what Borderland Theology might look like today.

The book's conclusion will present some final examples and underscore the need for those who would be faithful to the Incarnation to find ways of continuing to embody this reality in their everyday lives. As we all know, sometimes crossing borders can be extremely scary and dangerous. Yet it can also be exhilarating and deeply enriching. As has wisely been said, this road is one that can only be made by walking. And there is no time like the present to begin.

My hope is that this book may be a contribution to Christian reflection by bringing the concepts of borders—and God's border-crossing examples—to the forefront. I believe that the Christian call to dissolve exclusionary and oppressive boundaries may be applied to borders of all kinds, be they national or geographic borders with all of their social, political and economic implications, or any number of other boundaries erected by human beings that stand in the way of the reconciling and healing love of God. Moreover, I believe the way we understand and respond to the borders separating us from each other will largely determine the shape the world takes in the years to come. In fact it may be the pivotal point around which the dilemmas being created by the global economy can be resolved.

Some years back there was a movie entitled "The Man Who Fell to Earth" starring David Bowie. Although it eventually degenerated into something of an FBI thriller, during its early scenes this film was deeply moving in its portrayal of the experience of coming to earth from an alien's point of view. The alien had learned English from television broadcasts picked up on his planet. He landed in the New Mexico desert and sought to slip into American society incognito in order to amass a fortune for the building of a space ship with which to bring people from his planet to earth.

The opening scenes were nearly without a sound track. One felt a tremendous amount of tension building up in the alien as he prepared to utter his first words to a woman to whom he sought to sell a gold ring at a pawn shop. He had hundreds of these rings and used them to secure a financial base of operations. These early scenes moved very slowly and this contributed to the strong sense of isolation experienced by the alien. Of course, David Bowie's portrayal of the alien accentuated the spooky ambiance of the film. His ability to project the feelings of an "outsider" was powerful, indeed.

I have often reflected on this film in relation to the Christian notion of Incarnation, seeking to gain some understanding of how Jesus must have felt finding himself among beings who not only did not appreciate him and his message, but who actually despised and rejected both. As one who had "fallen to earth," seeking to explain himself and his mission to humankind, he surely experienced a great deal of frustration, rejection, and alienation. Clearly, Jesus was a "man without a country," a truly "displaced person."

In unguarded terms I am arguing that in several senses Jesus is portrayed in the Gospel accounts as having been an "undocumented alien" during his sojourn here on earth. Not only did he cross many borders throughout his three year ministry, such as those between Judea and Samaria, Galilee and Jerusalem, and Israel and various Canaanite communities, but he was always something of an "outsider" in relation to his own relatives, neighbors, and even his own disciples. From the first he was a marked man among the religious leaders of his time and place, and in the end they did him in.

At yet a deeper level we can recognized that Jesus was an "undocumented alien" in a cosmic sense as well. For, according to the Christian notion of Incarnation, he initially crossed the boundary between the transcendent dimension of reality and the natural dimension in which humans dwell. As John has it: "The Word became flesh and dwelt among us.... and we beheld his glory...full of grace and truth...He came unto his own and his own received him not." Or as Paul expresses it: "He humbled himself and became even as a servant" of those to whom he came to minister.

It is my contention that in the Christian concept of the Incarnation resides the deepest understanding, not only of God's investment in humanity—Immanuel—but of what it means for would-be disciples to be faithful to that investment. God came among us as an "undocumented alien," taking up the cause of those who are oppressed. Can we do any less? God would seem to dwell "at the border" and invites those who seek to be faithful to do likewise.

Part One:

The Bible and

the Borderlands

1

The Incarnational Paradigm

The Word Became Flesh

The basic claim of the Christian Faith is that "God was in Christ reconciling the world." The crucial word here is "in" and, put in theological terms, this pivotal idea involves what is called the "Incarnation," or the enfleshment of Divine Reality in human form. The idea is also captured nicely by the Hebrew term 'Immanuel' or "God with us."

Down through the centuries the Christian Church, and various thinkers within it, have wrestled with and argued over the precise meaning of this claim. Many church councils and hundreds of books have sought to focus on the diverse implications of the Christian notion of Incarnation.

In general there are two extremes to the debate. On the right are those who believe that God only *appeared* to become flesh in Jesus Christ. In the early centuries, these folk were called *docetists* after the Greek term meaning "to appear," and were rejected as heretics. Many people, however, believe this even today. In an effort to stress the divinity of Christ they end up denying his humanity. I call this the "Clark Kent" view of the Incarnation because it sees Christ as a Superman only pretending to be a mild-mannered carpenter from Nazareth. These people verbally affirm loyalty to the idea of the humanity of Christ, but for all practical purposes they worship Christ as exclusively divine.

On the left there are those who believe that God was in Christ in much the same way as God is potentially in all of us, and that this potential was especially actualized in Jesus of Nazareth. Christ is seen as essentially a wise and good moral teacher, much like Socrates, Gandhi, St. Francis, Martin Luther King, Jr., Helen Keller, or St. Theresa. In my opinion, those who espouse this view fail to do justice to the radical quality of the Christian Gospel by short changing the transcendent character of the person of Christ.

Fully Human and Fully Divine

Somewhere in between these two views there exists a more holistic perspective that integrates both Christ's divinity and his humanity. It is not a dualistic or schizophrenic interpretation of Jesus Christ as a kind of cosmic Dr. Jekyll and Mr. Hyde, but rather a view of Jesus Christ as an integrated person, a view I believe is true to the New Testament witness.

In the biblical accounts of Jesus' activities there are no references to any division between his divinity and his humanity. When he weeps or is thirsty, we are not told that this reflects his humanness. Nor when he heals the sick are we told that this expresses his divinity. In other places, such as his internal struggle in the Garden before his crucifixion, when he prays "Not my will but Thine," Jesus is a unified being, neither strictly divine nor merely human. [Matthew 26:39]

However difficult it may be to imagine the psychological implications of a fully divine yet fully human being, the fact remains that Jesus is presented in the New Testament as one who integrates these two dimensions of reality in a single person. There are instances of his being transfigured, on the one hand, and others of his being deeply frustrated, on the other hand, but in every case Jesus is just who he is—one who somehow crosses, even disintegrates, the barrier between the divine and the human.

All of this is especially relevant to the idea of the Incarnation in relation to a "divine border crossing." Both of the previously mentioned extreme views essentially eliminate the idea of divine border crossing at the outset since they each limit Jesus Christ to one side or the other of the divine-human distinction. In addition, the dualistic view also cancels out the notion of "divine border crossing" by virtue of its inability to connect the divine and human in Jesus Christ in anything like a holistic, integrated way.

I would argue for an understanding of the Incarnation as a Divine Reality, fully present and active in a human person without overriding the integrity of that person. To employ a chemical metaphor borrowed from Sallie McFague, the divine must be seen as continuously "in solution" without residue in the liquid of humanity in order for the Incarnation to be authentic. Or, to borrow from Henry James, by way of Flannery O'Connor, the divine mystery must always be mediated in and through the "manners" of everyday life.

In his well-known book, *Fear and Trembling,* Soren Kierkegaard speaks of the "Knight of Faith" as transcending the aesthetic, the ethical, and even the "religious" mode of existence by incorporating the divine into the human without any detectable trace of a line of demarcation between them. He employs the fascinating image of the ideal ballet dancer who is able to transform a leap into the air into a graceful walk with absolutely no hint of a jolt when returning to the ground. Here is an image of the Incarnation that truly does justice to the witness of the New Testament and to the notion of "divine border crossing" at the same time.

This view of Incarnation or divine border crossing is actually inherent within the early chapters of the Judeo-Christian scriptures where God is said to have breathed into humanity "the breath of life" and to have made us in the divine "image." In these passages resides a great mystery concerning the nature of creation and the relation between the creator and the created world. [Genesis 1:27, 2:7]

When humans were brought or shaped into being, Divine Reality extended, infused, or transposed itself into human form, and gave birth to a fresh embodiment of itself. In so doing God ceased to be an independent being and became a *relational* one. God chose to enter into relationship with created reality and, like a parent, could no longer exist as a reality unto itself. A border had been crossed and there was no turning back.

The most straightforward presentations of the notion of the Incarnation in the Christian scriptures are in the Gospel of John and in Paul's letter to the Philippians. [Philippians 2:6-9] John begins his narrative with the statement, "In the beginning was the Word. The Word was with God and the Word was God." The Greek word for "word" is "Logos" and is here a designation for the divine "rationale" or "principle" that manifested itself in Jesus Christ. This term already had a long and well-known philosophical history in the Greco-Roman world, but John was giving it a special twist by connecting it up in this way with a particular human person, namely Jesus. In brief, he was saying that the cosmic principle of creation and life was somehow embodied in the man Jesus of Nazareth. The Logos had become flesh.

John also speaks of Jesus as the "light of the world" in this profound prologue to his Gospel. This light, he says, came "into the world" and "unto its own," but neither received nor comprehended it. Here we encounter the idea of "border crossing" quite directly. Indeed, the Divine Word not only infuses itself in to the human world, but when it does so it is treated as an alien, as an unwanted outsider. It is as if the one crossing the border was without documentation and was deemed an "illegal entrant."

This depiction of the world's rejection of the Word of God in the person of Jesus Christ puts one in mind of the passages in the latter chapters of Isaiah concerning the "Suffering Servant," such as "He was despised and rejected by humanity." [Isaiah 53:3] Here it is clear that even for God the business of crossing borders can be a risky and costly endeavor. In the Incarnation there is no guarantee that God will receive a warm welcome, indeed, as John puts it: "His own received him not." In short, the Word was neither understood nor accepted by humankind. We will return to this "unwanted alien" theme in subsequent chapters.

In the second chapter of Paul's letter to the church at Philippi we encounter what is called the "Kenosis passage." "Kenosis" is the Greek word that means "to empty" and in this passage it is stated that Christ Jesus, the divine Word, chose to empty himself of divine prerogatives and become a human being. Believers are here called on to embody the same humility of Christ when he set aside his own entitlements in order to bring God's love to humanity. He did not cling to the privileges pertaining to his superior station, but freely gave them up for our ultimate well-being.

Not only did God deign to become a human being, but we are told that he crossed the border into our realm in the form of a servant and even humbled himself to the extent of being willing to be murdered by those to whom he had come. And it was not just any death. This death by crucifixion was one generally reserved for criminals, the lowest of the low. This was the fate of the divine immigrant.

A present-day analogy may bring the importance of this passage home more forcefully. It frequently happens that refugees arriving in the United States from foreign lands are people of considerable training and experience in their home country, but when they come to us they have been stripped of these advantages. Much of this "humbling" is the result of not being able to function in a foreign language. But often the difficulties such persons face also result from different qualifying criteria relevant to the field of work they have been working in, such as law, medicine, and education.

At an even deeper level, however, lies the sort of difficulty such people encounter when they sense the rejection that mainstream U.S.-Americans dispense to anyone who speaks a language that is different from our own. Sometimes, if only subconsciously, English speaking people attribute an immigrant's accent or grammatical awkwardness to inferior intelligence or even to subversive intent. Often these "aliens" are forced to live in substandard housing, to take jobs that no one else wants, and to struggle trying to make friends. Far too frequently they actually are suspected and accused of crimes falsely and suffer dire consequences.

It is this sort of humbling that Jesus Christ suffered when he arrived on our human shores from the divine realm. He was rejected by his own family, neighbors, religious and political leaders, and even on occasion by his own disciples. Throughout his life, and especially in his death, he found it necessary to struggle against misunderstanding, suspicion, and outright hostility. He was truly a person without a country, one "with no place to lay his head." [Matthew 8:20]

The Risk of Rejection

Now comes the tough part. Christians are familiar enough with the idea of the Incarnation, but we generally fail to deal honestly with its implications. It's easy to view the whole thing as if it was all planned from the beginning by God and was simply acted out by the players involved so as to fulfill the divine plan. Some might say that even though Jesus Christ experienced rejection and suffering upon his entrance into our world, he knew all along that he would ultimately be reinstated to his rightful place and rewarded for carrying out his divine mission so successfully. We may celebrate the resurrected

Jesus—the winner—who is the center of a now powerful and widespread religion, without celebrating the Jesus who was poor, rejected, and despised.

In the same way, North Americans tend to embrace those immigrants like Einstein, Eli Wiesel, and sports stars from other continents, once they have made a name for themselves. Then we say that we are truly a great melting pot of ethnic diversity. All too quickly we forget the real injustices and shame immigrants have had to face, and still do face, here in white, Anglo-Saxon Protestant America. Vigilante groups and the latest polls reflecting anti-immigrant attitudes are testimony to the fact that for the most part, immigrants—like Christ—are "despised and rejected by humanity."

My own understanding of the issues involved here is not very traditional. As near as I can tell, both from these two crucial passages and from the way the Gospel writers present Jesus' life and teachings, the crossing of the border embodied in the Incarnation necessarily implied the crucial element of cosmic risk. That is to say, without the real possibility that this entire effort could end up in failure, the whole story reduces to a kind of farce, a cosmic puppet show, or a divine charade.

Just as is the case with all human immigrants, whether documented or not, there is no guarantee that they will not encounter suspicion, rejection, and even deportation when they attempt to cross a given border, so it is with the Incarnation. God could not provide some sort of cosmic "safety net" that would carry Jesus through the various difficulties he would face without undermining the basic purpose of the entire endeavor. If there was no genuine risk, no real possibility of failure, then of what value is Jesus' resolve and commitment to God's will?

There are two central passages of scripture in which this basic fact is powerfully dramatized. One is found in Matthew's fourth chapter where Jesus is confronted with three basic temptations. The driving force behind these temptations was the real possibility that Jesus could fall back on his privileged status and powers in order to make his mission a triumph. The meaning of Jesus' refusal to give in to these temptations pivots on the real possibility that he *could have*

The Incarnational Paradigm

yielded to them. Otherwise the point of the entire drama is reduced to cosmic theater.

The other passage that makes this point poignantly clear is the famous Garden of Gethsemane scene where Jesus is seen struggling with whether or not to go through with the process that will lead to his crucifixion. If it had not been possible for him to back out of this entire scenario, the scene would have been stripped of all of its drama and theological significance. The agony and sweat "as of great drops of blood" would be nothing but theatrics. The whole point of the resurrection revolves around the claim that Jesus *chose* to go through with this sequence of events. He could have done otherwise.

In the Philippians 2:6-9 passage, the force of the "Therefore" at the beginning of verse nine ("Therefore God has highly exalted him. . .") hinges on Jesus having been willing to risk everything in crossing the border into the human realm. *Because* he was faithful to God's call, he was honored and rewarded in the resurrection. Jesus' act of self humbling carried with it real and absolute risk; it was not merely the fulfillment of some divine plan that moved inexorably forward toward a predetermined end.

It is worth considering the possibility that even the writers of the New Testament themselves were unable to fully accept the real implications of Jesus' self humbling in the Incarnation. For often, as in this very passage in Philippians, they seem intent on emphasizing the ultimate vindication of Jesus as the mighty conqueror without giving serious regard to his consistent refusal to accept such kingly honor. To take the Incarnation seriously entails acknowledging this refusal.

This is precisely the issue raised by the scene in which Jesus sets out to wash the disciples' feet. Peter refuses on the grounds that the master must not wash the servants' feet; yet Jesus tells Peter that he is failing to grasp the radical character of his new message, namely that God is not interested in being the "master" but in being the "servant." The Incarnation amounts to a complete reversal of the usual human hierarchical categories of placing some above others. God not only crossed the border into humanity, but in doing so took on the form of a servant, not a master. Unfortunately the early church, like its modern counterpart, often forgot the radical nature of this message.

This same contradiction can be seen in the book of Revelation chapters 5 and 6 where the Lamb of God, the sacrificial servant who gave himself for the sins of the world, is not only praised as "worthy" but is portrayed as a vengeful and judgmental monarch who sits on a throne lording it over sinners and saints alike. It is difficult to smooth over the contrast between this image of Christ and that depicted in the Gospels. Surely the sort of "victory" accomplished in God's triumph will not involve the small and dictatorial posture symbolized in such images. Love will win out by means of persuasion, not force.

I believe that the significance of the Incarnation must not be erased by interpretations that sap it of its radical character. If there was no real risk involved in God's crossing the border into the human realm, no real vulnerability on God's part, then the whole story loses its power to transform our relation to God. It is God's willingness to suffer on our behalf that accomplishes our reconciliation.

The significance of Christ's resurrection is not to be found in some sort of physical and/or political conquest in which all God's enemies have been vanquished by sheer military force. The power inherent within the resurrection, as the early chapters of the Acts of the Apostles make clear, lies within the on-going activity of the Holy Spirit in the lives of those who choose to follow Christ. The resurrection is experienced in the midst of continuing struggle, not after or instead of it.

Christ's Border Crossing Ministry on Earth

There are several instances in the Gospel accounts of Jesus' life and teaching that bring this aspect of the Incarnation to the forefront. They are situations in which Jesus' insistence on crossing borders clearly demonstrates that such "immigration" was an essential aspect of his calling; that Jesus was not only incarnated into this world from the divine dimension, but that while in this incarnated form he consistently put himself at risk by crossing over various other human borders, whether geographic, ethnic, or religious.

Two of the clearest of these instances are where he crosses over the line with respect to Samaritans. We often fail to fully appreciate

The Incarnational Paradigm 17

the force of these stories because we do not know the historical and cultural background involved in the antipathy between Jews and Samaritans. When the Northern Kingdom of Israel was taken captive by the Assyrians around 721 B.C., many of the people were transported to other areas of the Assyrian empire and were replaced by folks from these areas. Over the years these two groups of people intermarried and developed their own particular form of Judaism. Samaritans were despised by Jews as heretics and half-breeds, and the reverse was true as well.

Here we see the importance of Jesus' needing to go through Samaria. Faithful Jews always sought to bypass this area. Jesus deliberately crossed over this traditional border to show that God does not play favorites. The episode with the woman at the well [John 4:24] tells of the inclusion of those traditionally excluded. Jesus clearly says that it is high-time such arbitrary theological and ethnic boundaries were set aside, for "those that worship God must do so in spirit and in truth."

In this same passage it is also significant that Jesus was setting aside the traditional border between men and women that was deeply ingrained in most traditional societies. No self-respecting Jewish male in Jesus' day would be caught dead speaking to a woman in public, let alone to one of "tainted" reputation. But Jesus consistently crossed over this sexist barrier, in this instance and in many others, to make it clear that in the Incarnation God was fully engaged in the business of reconciliation on all levels.

Here, too, we see the full significance of the story of the Good Samaritan. [Luke 10:20-36] It was not simply that this fellow was willing to be of help to someone in need; In a surprising twist, Jesus made the hero of this story a Samaritan in order to stress the radical role reversal implied by the Incarnation. This surprising twist to his story challenged the anti-Samaritan racism of the time and challenges us today to break down our modern-day barriers and prejudices towards people of other races and ethnicities. In the Incarnation all barriers are crossed.

The story of the Syro-Phoenician woman who begged Jesus to heal her daughter once again shows how Jesus refused to be boxed in by traditional borders. [Mark 7:26-30] Not only did he accept her faith as greater than anything he had seen among the orthodox Jews, even though she was clearly a "pagan" in their eyes, but he was astounded by her own ability to see beyond the racist terminology the Jews employed for Gentile "dogs."

Jesus displayed this same disregard for conventional categories in his dealings with other disliked people such as prostitutes, compromising tax collectors, and even Roman leaders.

One last story should suffice to make this point. Remember when Jesus said to his disciples "Let's get into the boat and go over to the other side?" [Mark 4:35-5:17] They crossed the Sea of Galilee to the region of the Gaderenes people, a non-Jewish group of people who actually raised and traded pigs, a forbidden food for Jews. Here again we see Jesus overlooking cultural barriers, including those that pertain to the labels people put on those who are afflicted with mental and emotional illnesses. Yet another border gets crossed.

During the last week of his life Jesus crossed the border that separated Judea and Jerusalem from the rest of Israel, especially his home region, Galilee. There he put himself at great risk in order to confront the religious and political powers of his day. Here again we see that "he came unto his own, but his own received him not." These leaders were all very threatened by his presence and his teaching because he came in an untraditional form and manner; he came with a message of love, honesty, and inclusiveness, setting aside hierarchies and pretenses.

As John put it in the first chapter of his Gospel, "He dwelt among us full of grace and truth." This dwelling was no mere appearance or virtual reality, it was the real thing. To claim that God became human flesh is to claim that God is in the business of eliminating borders at both the cosmic and cultural levels.

Reconciliation: The Goal of Border Crossing

In Paul's letters there are at least three key passages that warrant discussion. The first involves the statement, "God was in Christ reconciling the world." [II Corinthians 6:19] It is important to note that in Paul's mind it is not God who is being reconciled to us, but we who are being reconciled to God and by extension to one another.

The Incarnational Paradigm   19

God's work in Christ was done for humanity's sake, not God's. The atonement seeks to put us at one with God.

The operative word in Paul's statement is, "reconciling." This term focuses the central concern of the Gospel of Christ, namely the overcoming of all barriers that separate people from God and vice versa. It also implies that God and humans are initially in "conciliation," or at one with each other, but that human distrust separates us from God, thereby requiring a reconciliation. To be an agent of reconciliation necessarily entails crossing the borders that divide beings from one another or building bridges over and between them. All attempts at reconciliation run the risk of being misunderstood and rejected.

Another important passage in Paul's writings that speaks of divine border crossing is Romans 5:8 which states that "While we were yet sinners Christ died for us." This statement contradicts the deeply ingrained notion that the reconciling work of God in Christ somehow depends on our having deserved it, on God meeting out rewards and punishments "fairly" in accordance with our relative merits. Paul flatly claims that God took the initiative in the work of reconciliation, not waiting until we had "shaped up" or even repented. Thus God's good favor was not a *result* of Christ's reconciling work, since it was God who made the first move. Christ came *because* God loved us, not the other way around.

The dynamics of divine reconciliation can be illustrated on the human level by reminding ourselves of the way "making up" works between friends or lovers. As long as we sit around trying to figure out who owes whom an apology, nothing ever really happens to overcome our mutual estrangement. Not until one person sets blame-placing aside and decides to go ahead and say, sincerely, "I'm sorry" does reconciliation begin to occur. The real gift in this dynamic is to be able to say "I'm sorry" even when your apology is not called for.

This is how it is with God's reconciling activity in the Incarnation; God does not wait around for us to say we are sorry but simply goes ahead and forgives us. It's almost as if God steps up and says," Oh, what the heck, I'm sorry." God *initiates* the reconciliation process rather than holding back until we take the responsibility for our estrangement.

A third set of passages relevant to our theme is where Paul speaks of the community of believers as the "body of Christ." [I Corinthians 12] Paul saw the Incarnation as being carried out in the life of the Christian community. If that is so, then the Incarnation was not a once-and-for-all event but is rather an on-going process that extends throughout the history and life of the church under the inspiration and guidance of the Holy Spirit.

Paul speaks of a body where Christ is the head, a directing presence that continues to incarnate in the body of believers. The believers are mutually interdependent and interactive parts of that body. Paul's understanding of the role of the body in an Incarnational view of the church is focused sharply in the first two verses of the twelfth chapter of his letter to the Romans. There he states that our reasonable worship involves presenting "our bodies as living sacrifices"—not our *souls* but our *bodies*, and not as dead sacrifice but as living ones. Christian faith means very little, according to Paul, if it is not embodied in the everyday life of believers.

The Challenge of Discernment

Finally, I'd like to say that the kind of border crossing represented in the Incarnation—the crossing from the divine to the human reality—is not a straightforward sort of thing. The Incarnation of God's love and wisdom was accomplished in and through the everyday details of Jesus' life and teaching. And while Jesus' words and actions can not be regarded as proof of God's direct action on our world, they can be understood as mediators of special significance—signs that God is with us.

Sometimes it takes a certain amount of discernment and reflection after the fact or during great uncertainty to recognize God's presence among us. In Luke 24 when the two disciples encountered the resurrected Jesus on the road to Emmaus, at first they failed even to recognize him. They began to inform him about the recent events in Jerusalem, and they did not recognize him even when he explained the scriptures to them. Only after he blessed and broke bread with them were their eyes opened to the reality of his presence. Then they saw the significance of the inner warmth that they felt in conversation with their risen Lord.

The Incarnational Paradigm 21

This is how the on-going community of believers has and will continue to discern the presence and activity of God in our midst, through a glass darkly [I Corinthians 13:12] and after the fact. It involves a large degree of mystery and open-endedness, as well as great risk and vulnerability. It may also involve following the example of Christ and crossing the borders set up to exclude others. The final two chapters of this book will present examples of people in Mexico and in the United States who, like Christ, have *crossed* lines and put their lives *on* the line.

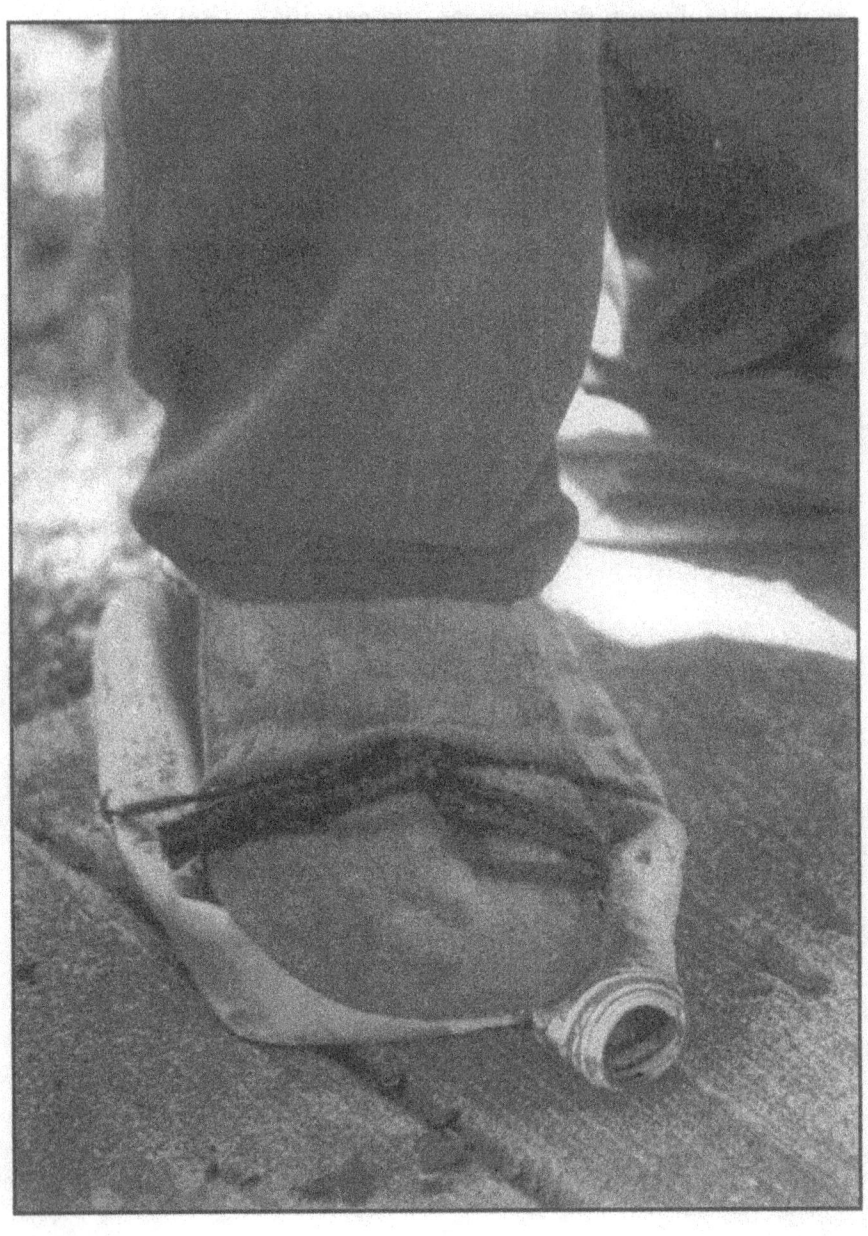

2

The Hebrew Scriptures

Outsiders and Insiders

Understanding the Incarnation as a cosmic border crossing enables one to see and appreciate the stories of the Hebrew Scripture—what Christians now call the Old Testament—in a whole new light. We can see the Hebrew people, for example, as a wandering and besieged people of God who are continuously crossing various borders, whether by choice or by force. The meaning of their actions, and thus of the stories themselves, is largely defined by these very borders.

In this chapter I will briefly review the history of the Hebrew people as it unfolds in their scripture with an eye to understanding the significance of borders and border crossings at the center of their story. From Genesis through the books of the law, the kings, and the prophets we can see that the notion of "the border" factors heavily into the nearly every story. Coming to understand this perspective can greatly enhance our recognition and appreciation of the nature of God's activity in the human world.

The Garden of Eden

Consider the context of the first human story in the Hebrew Scripture, that of the Garden of Eden. [Genesis 3] The entire drama of this story hinges on the role played by the boundary that God set up around the Tree of the Knowledge of Good and Evil. Whatever else one can say about the meaning of this story, and it surely does leave a great deal of room for interpretation, it cannot be denied that the character of Adam and Eve, and of human nature in general, pivot on the fact that they chose to cross this boundary, this border.

This border crossing was viewed as a transgression or trespassing, and the result was that Adam and Eve were driven by God across yet another border out of the Garden of Eden. The most significant theological point of this drama is that after having expelled the couple from the Garden, God was not content to remain in the Garden in a self-righteous huff but rather followed Adam and Eve, and eventually their offspring Cain and Abel, into the world in order to continue to interact with them as they set about to employ this new found capacity to choose between good and evil.

Outside the Garden, Adam and Eve could no longer interact directly with God, however. They became "outsiders" who were then forced to relate to God in a mediated fashion. They entered the human world as refugees from another place, no longer living in harmony with their surroundings. As outsiders in a new place, they and their children undoubtedly would have experienced a good deal of alienation and feelings of displacement as they began their life together at a distance from God.

God did not abandon them or denigrate them as immigrants or exiles but rather sought them out and strove to reestablish a relationship with them. Even though things did not go well, as in the case of the Flood [Genesis 6] and the Tower of Babel [Genesis 11], there was continuous interaction between God and humanity, as well as between various peoples of the earth. After the Flood, for instance, Noah and his family arrived in what was tantamount to a new world altogether and once again had to make their way as strangers in a strange land. Displacement and relocation across borders was a constant feature in the stories of these early peoples on the earth. And God, too, was an active agent in the midst of these on-going border crossings.

The degree to which borders and the crossing of them figures into these early stories of the Hebrews generally goes unnoticed, and the fact that God continues to follow these folks around picking up the pieces also usually goes unnoticed. Yet it is precisely this refusal to stay on the other side of the various boundaries separating people from one another and from God that comes to characterize the Divine Reality at the heart of the Hebrew faith.

Abraham, Jacob, and Joseph
When we shift to the more truly historical stories in the Hebrew Scripture, after the twelfth chapter of Genesis, we begin to see an even

greater role played by borders. In fact, in some ways the entire story of the Jewish people unfolds as a saga of wandering and displacement, even as their modern history has been. Though they have continuously sought a land of their own, and have on occasion possessed one, the basic story line of their existence has been and continues to be one of seeking rather than of having found their real home.

Upon leaving his home in Ur of the Chaldees, Abraham immediately became nomadic, or as we might say today, a migrant. Thus, throughout their travels to Haran and Egypt by way of Canaan, Abraham and his family were continuously outsiders. That is to say, they were almost always on the wrong side of the various borders they happened to encounter, and the citizens of the lands they traversed strongly resisted their presence. [Genesis, Chapters 12 -50] Ironically, even as many Christians have little compassion for the migrants among us today, these founders of the Judeo-Christian faith, whom we extol for their courage and persistence, were themselves migrants.

At first Abraham and his family settled in Canaan as distinct outsiders and had to make their own way among those living there. It seems that they were somewhat successful at this for several generations, during which time his son Isaac and grandson Jacob traveled a great deal up and down the land making alliances and securing wives. One of the most moving and insightful stories in the whole of Hebrew scripture is that of the reuniting of Jacob and Esau after Jacob had bilked Esau out of nearly everything that was rightfully his. Here again we see people coming together across psychological and spiritual borders, as well as physical ones.

During his own wanderings, Jacob himself had twice been visited by God. The first time he had a vision of a ladder that reached from heaven to earth and upon which God's angels were moving from place to place. [Genesis 28: 10-17] This was an extremely important experience for Jacob, for it indicated that God had not left him strictly to his own efforts but continued to be active in his life. Indeed, here was yet another instance in which God was extended across the border between humans and divine reality. Quite literally God had bridged the gap or boundary that normally separates these two realms.

The second of Jacob's encounters with God took place as he was preparing to meet his estranged brother Esau. [Genesis 32: 22-31] During the night Jacob was engaged by an angel who forced him to wrestle for many hours in order to change his name from Jacob, which means "supplanter" or "wrestler with humans," to Israel, which means "wrestler with God." Here, too, we see God taking the initiative to cross the border that Jacob had set up between himself and God in order to effect a change of character in Jacob.

Later on, Jacob's sons sold their young brother Joseph into slavery in Egypt out of spite for the way their father favored him. Joseph fared better in Egypt than your average displaced person and actually became a special favorite of the Pharoah. He even was able to discern the activity of God in the midst of what started out as a great misfortune.

When the whole land fell upon hard times, Jacob eventually sent his sons across the border into Egypt in search of livelihood, and there they encountered Joseph again. This time they found themselves as the outsiders begging for the mercy from their own brother whom they did not recognize.

But Joseph did not wait around until his brothers who had betrayed him had asked for his forgiveness. He simply received them with open arms and found a way to help them and his father who was waiting at home. In short, Joseph took the high road in this situation, overcoming the barrier between himself and his brothers by initiating their reconciliation. He put his own hurt aside and forgave them.

I want to point out again that whenever someone takes the initiative to step across the boundaries that cause or represent estrangement they place themselves at great risk. Not only do they risk rejection by the person they are reaching out to, but there is also a special sort of vulnerability in taking the first step toward reconciliation because such a step tacitly implies that one is somehow the guilty party. To make this move is somewhat like saying "I'm sorry" even though you did not cause the separation.

Because Joseph was able to experience the presence of God even in a strange land, he was also able to receive and forgive his brothers when they appeared before him. They were all able to successfully cross these respective borders and boundaries because God, too, had done so.

It seems to me that this is one of the most extraordinary and deeply moving aspects of divine activity as portrayed in the Judeo-Christian scriptures. Throughout the Hebrew story God is seen as continually pursuing the Jewish people, trying to persuade them to return to a vital relationship with the divine. In each case it is God who takes the initiative, even though it is Israel that repeatedly turns from following the divine way and severs the relationship established by their covenants with God. It is always God who steps across this breech in their relationship, as if to say "Let's put this separation behind us. It doesn't matter who's to blame."

Because of Joseph, Abraham's descendents were provisionally accepted within the boundaries of the Egyptian empire in their time of great need. But while living in their adopted locale, they prospered to such an extent that they came to be seen as a threat by the Egyptian leaders, and they were placed under severe oppression as slave laborers. [Exodus 1 and 2, Exodus 3-40] Once again they were seen as migrants and outsiders who had overstayed their welcome, and they began to cry out for help and deliverance.

In much the same way, immigrants in the United States have experienced cycles of welcome and rejection. While the economy is booming or when low-wage labor is needed, the United States has historically been more tolerant of immigrants, sometimes even recruiting migrant labor. Chinese workers were brought to work on the railroads in the 1880s and 1890s, for example, and a *bracero* program that recruited Mexican farm workers was in effect from 1942 to 1964. Yet, when people feel threatened economically or politically, once again the laws change, immigration raids begin, and immigrants are deported or forced into the slavery of clandestine work.

The Exodus

In the well-known story of the Exodus God called Moses to lead the Hebrew people beyond the barriers of slavery to a new land of their own. He led them across the borders of Egypt into the Sinai desert and again they became nomadic migrants whom no one else wanted in their land. On their way to the promised land they encountered repeated hostility from all those peoples with whom they came in contact. Their path led them across the borders of Edom, Moab, and Ammon to whom they were a threat and against whom they had to wage war in order to be able to pass through their respective territories.

As we can see, some border crossings are hostile and point to the fact that borders are at times necessary to protect people from their enemies. Here it is necessary to distinguish between borders being crossed by needy people looking for a home and borders that are invaded by powerful forces for purposes of conquest and domination. At times the aggressive manner by which the Hebrews made their way to the Promised Land renders their cause and efforts less sympathetic.

It is not a large leap, however, to think of today's immigrants to the United States as a modern day Hebrew people, driven by hunger and oppression in their own countries to look for a home where they can make a living with dignity. Is it possible that the undocumented peoples among us are a unique, "chosen people" of God? Is it possible that in welcoming unwanted outsiders, we are "entertaining angels unaware?" What does seem clear is that God crosses borders with them and is present among them.

Eventually the Hebrew people were led into the land of Canaan by Joshua and proceeded to conquer the local inhabitants who were dwelling there. Here we have an astonishing turn around, for now those who were outsiders have become insiders and they in turn treat the former insiders as outsiders. The borders get crossed and new boundaries are set up between the different tribal groups involved. Today such an invasion would be subject to criticism, and hopefully people of faith would consider the suffering of those invaded. It remains perfectly clear, nevertheless, that the borders between geographical areas and peoples constitute the context or arena within which the dramas of the Hebrew scriptures are played out. Sociopolitical factors are as crucial to the meaning of the story as the events and characters that make the plot.

Once established in their promised land, the Hebrews had to struggle continuously to maintain their own borders against the onslaughts of various would-be invaders, such as Egypt and Assyria.

The Hebrew Scriptures

These two empires frequently sought to conquer the Hebrews, essentially ignoring the borders that had been set up between them. They both forced the Hebrews to pay high taxes for the privilege of existing on this narrow strip of land that served as the highway for their respective war efforts. In essence, the Jewish people served as the fifty yard line, or better still the football itself, in the conflicts between and among the surrounding countries.

Finally, Saul, David, and Solomon were somewhat successful in stabilizing the situation and providing the Hebrew people with various brief periods of relative peace. Actually the great "Davidic Kingdom" only lasted about thirty years. Solomon was only able to keep his kingdom going by entering into various marriages with the princesses of several nearby nations.

Not long after Solomon's death, the kingdom was split into two parts, the northern kingdom of Israel and the southern kingdom of Judea. [II Kings 12] Now in addition to the borders that separated the Hebrews from their enemies, there was one that separated them from themselves. The different kings of these two groups waged any number of battles against each other over a number of decades. This was the time of the prophets, both major and minor, among the Hebrew people. These spokespersons for God consistently urged the people to worry less about their neighbors and more about their relationship to the divine. An especially important principle, however, was that being in a right relationship with God meant "doing justice" in relation to the poor and the oppressed in and among their people.

Naomi and Ruth

Before discussing the two exile experiences of the Hebrew people in foreign lands, let us look at the book of Ruth. The story is set in the time of the Judges, soon after the conquest of Canaan by Joshua and his followers. It is unclear when, why and by whom the book of Ruth was written, and it seems completely out of sync with the events and quality of life presented in the book of Judges which purportedly records the history of that period, for its emphasis is primarily on peace and inclusiveness.

The subtext of the book of Ruth revolves around the issues of borders and their respective insiders and outsiders. The Jewish people had always been outsiders during their many sojourns from Haran to Egypt, through the desert and into the land of Canaan. Once they established themselves in the land, however, the tables were turned and they then became the insiders struggling against other outsiders who were seeking to overrun or control them from the outside. In the story of Naomi and her daughter-in-law Ruth, however, we see this whole scenario folded back on itself.

What is especially interesting about this story is how it focuses the reconciling and redemptive aspects of borders and foreigners, of immigrants and migrants. For here we encounter people traveling back and forth across traditionally hostile borders who are nonetheless capable of genuine and deep acceptance of one another. Perhaps this story was meant to teach the Hebrews something that much of the rest of their history belies.

Naomi and her family emigrated from Judah to Moab during a time of famine. The historical and political context of this situation is significant here. Not only had the Hebrew people fought their way through the Moabites on their way to the land of Canaan, but ever after they regarded them as hopeless pagans. And yet now, in a time of great adversity, they were willing to go and live among the Moabites in order to make a new life.

So here we have Naomi and her family as refugees among a people whom they supposedly despised. Not only that, but they apparently felt comfortable enough among these folks for the two sons to marry Moabite women. Surely such behavior would have raised more than a few moralistic eyebrows back home in Canaan. Intermarriage with foreigners was very much forbidden among the Hebrews, but here is a family of the faithful who somehow were able to rise above such narrowness and extend the blessing of God's grace to include traditional outsiders.

When times got tough in Moab, after Naomi's two sons had died, she decided to return to her homeland. The best known part of the story is that the Moabite daughter-in-law, Ruth, decided to accompany Naomi. She expressed this decision in the strong language of her famous commitment: "Wither thou goest I shall go.... and thy God shall be my God." It takes only a moment's reflection to see what a momentous decision this was, since not only was she about to enter a strange land but one in which she would be regarded as a pagan and enemy. Here again we see the dynamics of this story carrying us across the customary lines of demarcation between insiders and outsiders.

Upon entering the land of Judah, Naomi and Ruth were both accepted into the Hebrew community. Ruth was allowed to glean in the fields according to the Jewish law that required harvesters to leave the corners of the fields unharvested so that the poor would have opportunity to acquire food. In reality, then, Ruth was not only a refugee among the Hebrew people, she was a migrant worker. This would have been an excellent chance for those working with her to treat her poorly, say that she didn't belong or that she didn't deserve to be there.

However, we are told that the local Hebrew people accepted Ruth for the person she was and treated her with kindness. Indeed, there is even a romantic dimension to this warm and inclusive story, as Boaz befriends Ruth and eventually takes her to be his wife. Here again we encounter the issue of intermarriage between Jews and "pagans," but this does not seem to have caused any difficulty in this particular case. The tone of the entire story is one of acceptance and inclusiveness on the part of the faithful. Refugees and traditional enemies are reconciled.

There is an additional feature of this story that often goes unnoticed. By being incorporated into the Hebrew people, Ruth became an important link in the genealogical lineage of Jesus himself. Just as Christians often conveniently forget that Jesus was a Jew, so Jews and Christians alike frequently fail to acknowledge that the ancestry of both King David and Jesus included a Moabite refugee. Everything about this story of Ruth contributes to its overall theme of inclusiveness and reconciliation among those traditionally regarded as enemies. Ruth was a refugee from a very foreign and hostile land, and yet she, like we, was reconciled to God and to those seeking to be faithful to God's grace.

The hard core of the Gospel of Christ is primarily about accepting those who have traditionally been placed outside of the blessing of divine reality. From God's perspective this acceptance is meant to incorporate all humankind into the household of faith, while from the perspective of those of us who would be participants in this faithful family such acceptance is meant to be characteristic of every aspect of our life together. Our reconciliation to God and to one another does not become effective *after* we have become faithful disciples, but serves as the very center of such discipleship.

It also seems that Naomi is a Christ figure in this story. It is, after all, Naomi who initially crosses the border between the "chosen ones" and the outcast Moabite. It is Naomi who receives Ruth into her family, making an outsider into an insider, without thought to the cost and risk involved. And it is Naomi, after assuring her of her free choice in the matter, who leads Ruth back to her original homeland, to a rich and peaceful life.

One of the most marginal groups of outsiders in our Western culture has always been women. Yet here it is Naomi who functions as the reconciling agent between the Hebrews and the Moabites at the general level and between Boaz and Ruth at the individual level.

So, not only does the story of Ruth teach us a great deal about the value of crossing borders that separate one group of people from another, it also instructs us about the importance of crossing boundaries and barriers that divide cultural subsets from each other. Unfortunately, we, like the Hebrews, have historically been slow to learn such lessons.

The Exiles

Returning now to the on-going record of the Hebrew as a nation, the exiles loom large in Jewish history. [II Kings 16-25, Daniel, Ezekiel, Ezra, Nehemiah] Around the year 721 B.C.E., the Assyrian empire overran the Northern Kingdom of Israel, deporting vast numbers of people to various other recently conquered lands to the East and importing many folks from those other lands into the Northern area of Palestine. Now the borders of this region were completely altered, as were the different populations. Over the next several hundred years the people in this northern region intermarried and developed a faith that limited itself to that of Abraham and Moses. The Jews of the Southern Kingdom of Judah came to see them as both impure half-breeds and heretics.

It was not too long, however, before Babylonia conquered the Assyrians and then in 586 B.C. took over the Southern Kingdom of Judah as well. The Babylonian policy was to completely remove their conquered enemies from their homelands so as to minimize the possibility of any political uprisings. The people of Israel were taken to Babylon and their homeland was left desolate. Only fifty years later, however, Persia conquered Babylon and in 536 B.C. they allowed the Hebrews to return home.

The people of the Northern Kingdom of Israel had been absent for 150 years and were no longer identifiable as a distinct people, and thus have generally been referred to as the "Ten Lost Tribes of Israel." Those Jews who did manage to return to their homeland after the Babylonian captivity had learned to "sing a new song by the waters of Babylon." [Nehemiah 1 and 2] They had learned to adjust to their strange and hostile situation, a lesson that has stood their people in good stead down through the centuries of their wandering and continued persecution. Adapt and survive became their practical motto, although they did not give up their unique social and religious heritage.

Upon their return to Palestine, these Hebrews worked at rebuilding Jerusalem and their culture, both of which centered around the Temple that Solomon had built and that their captors had destroyed. They were partially successful at this rebuilding project, but they never were able to reestablish their own sovereignty as a nation. Right down to the Roman occupation of the Holy Land, with which the Christian Scriptures begin, they were almost continuously under the heel of outside powers, such as Syria and Greece.

God Calls for Justice and Accompanies the Outsiders

So, whether they were in their own land or in some one else's, the Hebrews were usually on the losing side of the insider-outsider equation. One of the dominant themes of the entire story from Genesis to Malachi is the oppression and displacement of the Hebrew people at the hands of other powers whether from the inside or the outside. Since they were nearly always in such dire straits, one of the main emphases that emerges from their story is that God is at work on behalf of those who cry out in great need, that God cares about both insiders and outsiders when they are oppressed and exploited. The question of justice is continually at the center of the drama of the Hebrew Scriptures.

For these reasons it is all the more surprising that in contemporary times we Christians, who seek to honor and learn from the Hebrew Scriptures, often seem to have very little understanding of or compassion for those who are in one way or another different from us. As today's insiders, we frequently treat newcomers and poor people pretty much the way that others treated the Hebrews in biblical times. We call them "gypsies," "vagrants," "wetbacks," etc. and often seek to limit their participation in our society while clearly profiting from their labor whenever it is convenient.

I would like to close this chapter by focusing on yet one further aspect of the insider-outsider theme in the Hebrew Scriptures and that is the relationship among the various groups *within* the Jewish nation. Even though the law was from the beginning especially clear and adamant about the fact that there were to be no second-class citizens among the Hebrew people, it was not long before class divisions began to arise.

One obvious division was between the priestly classes of the Levites and the sons of Aaron, who were in charge of the rules and practices that governed religious ritual and ceremonies. It became easy and "natural" for such persons to lord it over and exploit the lay folk. In addition, it was not long before the people begged for a king so they could be like the other nations around them. Although their religious leaders were reluctant to give in to this request they did so, and thus a new type of class division was set in motion. The kings began to manipulate the interests of the people to conform to their own interests. Many treaties were made and wars fought in order to preserve and serve the interests of the royalty. Much of the history of the Jewish nation was characterized by a rapid succession of rulers, each no better than and often worse than the previous ones.

As with any group of people, there was also a division between the rich and the poor. The latter were made up of widows, orphans, the sickly, the mentally disturbed, and prisoners. In spite of the fact that Jewish law made provision for such folks, these regulations were very rarely invoked and the streets were full of people who stood in great need. The rich, on the other hand, were largely made up of those who found it profitable to cooperate with the occupation forces of the Syrian, Greek, or Roman colonial powers. Their political connections made it possible for them to take full advantage of the less fortunate in their midst.

In the final years leading up to the Assyrian and Babylonian captivities the Hebrew prophets consistently reprimanded their leaders and the wealthy for failing to be faithful to the law and will of God by seeing to it that justice was done on behalf of the needy. They even declared that God was not as interested in the rituals and ceremonies as in the cause of justice. "I hate your feasts and sacred ceremonies...I will not accept your sacrifices and offerings...spare me the sound of your songs...let justice roll on like a river and righteousness like an ever-flowing stream." [Amos 5:21—24]

By the time we get to Jesus' day we find these divisions and injustices rampant. The disenfranchised have been fully marginalized while the religious and political leaders are taking full advantage of their privileged position and continually exploit the common people. They deliberately ignore the words of Micah 6:8: "God has told you what is good; and what is it that the Lord asks of you? Only to act justly, to love mercy, and to walk humbly with your God."

It is clear, then, that throughout the Hebrew Scriptures borders of all kinds played a significant part in the telling of the story of the Jewish people. There was constant interweaving of geographical, political, racial, and cultural borders around the goings and comings of the Hebrew nation. Often these various barriers between different people merged and overlapped, but the drama pivots around the business of deciding who is an insider and who is an outsider. It is the task of a Borderland Theology to examine the contours and implications of this phenomenon as it is found in both the Scriptures and in contemporary Christian society.

It is especially important to understand how an Incarnational approach to the issues revolving around the notion of borders can make a difference, both theologically and practically. If the Scripture is seen as God's concern and effort to overcome all those barriers that separate people from one another and from Divine Reality itself, then the urgency of this task takes on added significance.

Incarnational theology and faithfulness require that we address and work toward the resolution and transformation of the estrangement within our borders. It is not sufficient for Christian believers to openly acknowledge their commitment to God's presence in the life and work of Jesus and to endeavor to center their personal lives around that commitment. The divine purpose of the Incarnation is to infuse the whole world, and especially its disenfranchised peoples, with the love and grace of God. This means bringing an end to oppression and exploitation.

3

The Christian Scriptures

Insiders and Outsiders

In the last chapter we saw the Jewish people living largely as outsiders with respect to the various peoples they encountered, both in their sojourns and in their new-found homeland. This is the dominant story of the Hebrew Scriptures. In the present chapter our focus will be on the Christian story as it arose within and out of the Jewish culture. We will see that in the New Testament, too, relocation and displacement are central themes, that insider-outsider dynamics continue to define relationship among peoples, and that Jesus consistently crosses the barriers that exclude or oppress peoples.

The Boundaries of Christ's Time

Within the Jewish nation in first century Palestine, Christians were initially seen as outsiders, renegades who were twisting the traditional Jewish faith and thus needed to be weeded out. At the same time, however, the Roman Empire was occupying the entire region and ruling by oppression and exploitation. While technically the outsiders in this land, the Romans actually functioned as the insiders because they controlled nearly every aspect of the society, whether political, economic, legal, or even religious. The hierarchical boundaries imposed by this sort of imperialism were actually more rigid than those of geography.

In addition to this imperial socio-political hierarchy there was also the long standing religious hierarchy set up by the priestly class within Judaism. At the top of the hierarchy were the priests, along with certain interpreters of the law called the scribes, and the extremely conservative self-appointed "pure" practitioners of the law, the Pharisees. There were also more extreme groups: the Zealots on the left, who sought to overthrow the Romans, and the Essenes on the right, who withdrew to the desert to await the apocalyptic judgment of God.

In the midst of all this there were two additional groups rather caught in the middle between the various powers that be. These were the people who collaborated with the Roman occupational forces (the tax collectors, for instance) and the simple poor folk. Even here there existed a hierarchy of oppression and exploitation, for the former preyed upon the latter grievously on their way to squeezing out extra profit from their assigned tasks. At the lowest end of the social hierarchy were people like the Samaritans, those living in the no-man's land between the region of Jerusalem in the south and that of Galilee in the north.

In addition to these divisions, a strong antipathy between the northern and southern regions continued to exist. Those dwelling in and around Jerusalem conceived of themselves as culturally and religiously superior to those from other areas largely because they lived near the Temple of Solomon. The people in the region of Galilee, for their part, were biased against and suspicious of their southern "city slicker" counterparts. Once again, the typical hierarchies and borders between and among people remained in place; and there were always insiders and outsiders.

One final hierarchical boundary which permeated the Jewish world of the Christian Scriptures was the boundary between women and men. There is little question about the degree to which Jewish males kept their womenfolk under severe subjugation, regarding them as little more than child producers and home servants. Women were not allowed to be seen alone in public, were never spoken to except at home, and were sometimes locked up in their houses when the men went out. There were separate sections for men and women in the synagogue, and women were not allowed to take an active part in worship services.

It was into these hierarchical patterns that Jesus came preaching and practicing understanding, compassion, and justice, especially to those people against whom the entire society was stacked from the outset. He came as one who would cross, and even melt such oppressive and dehumanizing borders and barriers. According to the Christian notion of Incarnation, "God was in Christ reconciling the world..."

Jesus Crosses Borders

The story begins with Mary, a very young, unmarried woman who comes to believe that God has set her apart for a very special mission, to be the mother of the one who would embody God in the world of human beings, thereby fulfilling the hopes and purpose of the Jewish tradition. The arrogance of this insignificant female, who became pregnant out of wedlock, in the eyes of those who knew her, must have seemed prodigious. God's first move in the Incarnation was to disregard such barriers. [Luke 1]

The story continues with Mary and Joseph journeying from Galilee to Bethlehem and finding that there was no room for them in the inn. [Luke 2:1-7] This theme of outsiders being turned away, or at best being given a place among the animals by those who already possess the basic necessities of life is a recurring one in the Gospel stories about God's activity in transforming the Word into flesh.

At the Christmas season in the United States, white middle-class or otherwise "established" Christians read the story and feel compassion for the Holy Family, but may fail to reflect on the full implications of this story for our own time and place. If we do stop to think about the implications, the results may be disturbing. Just what is our typical response, for instance, to unwed mothers and the homeless persons who keep turning up on our sidewalks and parks? We may be more prone to disdain and anger than to compassion. Saying "Get a job" and "Just say no," have become common ways of dealing with people who represent what some consider "social problems." The same must be said for the way most of the people in our country treat the immigrants, migrants, and misfits among us. Why would our reception of Mary and Joseph have been any different?

In churches with a large number of Mexican or Central American immigrants, however, the identification with this Christmas story is different. Often church people will take part in a door-to-door procession that is a reenactment of the journey of Mary and Joseph looking for a place in the inn. As each door opens only to say there is no room, there is deep identification with a Jesus who needs a home. Sometimes these reenactments, called *Posadas*, are accompanied with a reflection about the situation of immigrants looking for a place in the United States.

The difficulty of finding a place for himself followed Jesus in later years as well. When Jesus began his teaching ministry he came to the people of Nazareth and Galilee. Later there were those who claimed that "nothing of value can come out of Nazareth." From the very start Jesus knew what it was like to be an outsider, for even his own neighbors argued that since he was one of them he had no right to try to teach them anything. "A prophet receives no honor from those in his own country." [Luke 4:24] Jesus' own family feared for his sanity and at least once sought to draw him away from his ministry. [Mark 3:21]

Crossing the border into Judea, Jesus found that things got even worse, for there he was not only a migrant from the North, a kind of "carpet-bagger," but he was challenging the power structure of the religious leaders as well. Once again we might remind ourselves that while Christians today admire and even worship Jesus because he stood up to the status quo, we have a tendency in our own society to judge and denigrate those who do so today. And while we like the fictional heroes in the movies and television who are frequently portrayed as fighting the system, we tend to view their real life counterparts with great suspicion and fear.

In the end, of course, Jesus was crucified as a common criminal and suffered humiliation at the hands of both the Roman and Jewish leaders. After the fact it is easy to say he was able to endure this because he was the Son of God, but it is difficult to believe that had we been on the scene in those days we would have acknowledged Jesus as Lord and savior instead of viewing him as a strange and dangerous man. This is generally the case with respect to all the heroes who fight for social change by crossing boundaries; after the fact we praise Martin Luther King and Mahatma Gandhi, but until they are "winners," they are regarded with suspicion and fear.

Jesus, however, is recorded as being exceedingly inclusive in his behavior toward those existing on the fringes of his society. In fact, Jesus reserved his strongest words of condemnation for the religious leaders of his day, while offering the highest praise for the various outsiders he encountered. In fact, it is possible to argue that the most distinctive thing about Jesus' life and teaching is the emphasis on the need to reach out to those who are generally ignored and mistreated in order to breakdown the traditional barriers and bring the love and grace of God into their lives.

Jesus Includes Women and Children

Let's consider some of the specific stories in the Gospels in order to make this point more vivid and concrete. In addition to the many occasions on which Jesus is depicted as healing and feeding large numbers of needy people, there are many, many stories in which he engages in direct interaction with particular individuals who in one way or another stand outside of the acceptable ranks of Jewish society. Time after time, Jesus directly crosses the standard borders between different classes of people and, by doing so, transforms or obliterates these borders.

There is the story of Jesus' encounter with the Syro-Phoenician woman while he and his disciples are traveling beyond the borders of Jewish territory. [Matthew 15:21-28, and Mark 7:24-30] Not only did the disciples not want to be bothered by this woman's insistent cry for help, but Jesus himself seems reluctant to pay her much attention.. His stance toward the woman seems puzzling if not downright racist. At first he reminds her that the grace of God is, like bread, for God's children and not for the "dogs," which is what the Jewish people called all those outside of their own faith. One might imagine Jesus making this remark with a twinkle in his eye, as if waiting to see how she would respond.

The woman does not appear to be offended by Jesus' seemingly racist remark, perhaps because she discerned that it was meant in a sort of rhetorical manner or perhaps because her desperation emboldened her. She simply says, "Even the dogs go after the crumbs that the children do not want." Jesus then makes a truly amazing statement, namely that in all of Israel he had not seen such faith. He was impressed with her wisdom, but he also recognized her faith, even though she was not a Jew.

So here we have Jesus crossing two borders at once, the border between Jews and Gentiles and the one between men and women. It is difficult for us today to appreciate the full significance of stories such as this, largely because we do not have quite the same set of cultural boundaries that the people of Jesus' day did. We do, however, have our own set and it is always valuable to spend some time reflecting on what these are and what we might do to overcome them. Racism and sexism, along with a number of other "isms," are still with us.

There are at least two other stories in the Gospels that deal with the issue of sexism. One is where Jesus encounters the Samaritan woman at the well [John 4] and the other is the one about the woman caught in the act of adultery. [John 8] In the first story, Jesus crosses two separate borders, the border between the Jews and the Samaritans and the one between males and females. Jesus is said to have gone deliberately through Samaria, even though orthodox Jews systematically avoided doing so, and to have engaged a woman in conversation in public. Each of these acts was a flat-out transgression of Jewish tradition.

The story of the woman taken in adultery repeats an emphasis common to Jesus' way of treating such issues and raises several important questions as well. One has to do with the very way the situation was set up. Just how does one arrange to "take" a woman in the act of adultery? Would it not be necessary to apprehend her male counterpart as well? Why was he not put on trial also?

Another important point is that it is clear from the way Jesus handled things that, to him, there were issues far more significant than those the Scribes and Pharisees were raising. In this instance he was cutting across the social boundaries or borders set up by the Mosaic Law, which specified that an adulterous woman should be stoned. It is similar to the situation where Jesus and his disciples were castigated for taking food from the field on the Sabbath Day. Jesus clearly valued human persons, including women, and their particular needs above the letter of the Law: "The Sabbath was made for people, not people for the Sabbath." [Mark 2:27] Condemnation was not part of Jesus' message, except when it came to the religious leaders of his day.

There are still other stories—about Mary, Martha, and Mary Magdalene, for example—that depict Jesus crossing the boundaries set between men and women. [John 11 and 12] We are also told that it was such women who were the first at the empty tomb on the morning of the Resurrection. The importance of the fact that Jesus counted

The Christian Scriptures

these women as his close friends and disciples in a time and culture that systematically excluded them can hardly be exaggerated.

Jesus also crossed borders in his openness toward little children. He scolded his disciples for trying to shoo away children who approached him, and said, "Let the children come to me and do not stop them, for the kingdom of heaven belongs to such as these." [Mark 10:14] This is a posture we might take for granted, but it was hardly the norm in that day. Indeed, children essentially had no rights at all in First Century Judaism and it is most likely that those whom Jesus gathered around himself on occasion were in fact orphans. He crossed this boundary as well.

Jesus Crosses the Barriers of Classism and Elitism

In many stories, Jesus is also seen cutting across class barriers. Jesus often associated with those who were designated as "sinners" by the religious leaders, and he upbraided the latter for their mistreatment of the former. On one such occasion he explained that any doctor must associate with the "sick" if they are to be healed, while the "healthy" have no need of a doctor. [Matt.; 9:10-13, Mark 2:15-17, and Luke 5:29-32] There are several levels of double entendre at work here, since it was the Pharisees who defined the religious reality within which these so-called sinners found themselves. Jesus simply turned the tables on these holier-than-thou types by pointing out that those who assume that they are "righteous" or "well" are really the ones who are sinful or "sick."

In all of the foregoing cases those who are generally regarded and treated as outsiders turn out to be insiders as far as Jesus is concerned. Samaritans, women, and so-called sinners are all included by him, while those who perceive of themselves as righteous and holy end up excluding themselves. Jesus' entire ministry can be understood as a parable in which God is trying to undercut the traditional human hierarchies that separate people from one another; not simply to put the last first and the first last, but to abolish all such distinctions entirely. We tend to love our hierarchies because they allow us to foist our own exclusionary values on the world around us, especially on those whom we do not like. But, the Good News is that all humans are loved by God and are viewed as "justified" or accepted in God's sight. By living this message, Jesus revealed the heart of God to humankind. This is also what got him killed.

There is one more story in which Jesus crosses the line between two entrenched traditional categories. It is worth mentioning for it has far reaching implications. In the account of Jesus washing the disciples' feet [John 13:1-20], we find him undercutting the familiar distinction between the master and his followers or servants. The common custom in a culture where folks wear only sandals is for the servant to wash the feet of the master or the guests upon their arrival in a house. In reversing this procedure, Jesus was serving notice that such hierarchies are irrelevant among those who wish to embody the love of God. The way of discipleship is the way of servanthood, even for the leader.

Peter was unable to accept this radical reversal of roles, and Jesus had to reprimand him for objecting to the whole procedure. In the same way, it has become apparent that neither the writers of some of the Christian Scriptures nor those who fashioned the structure of the Church down through the ages were able to assimilate the radical character of Jesus' message. A good number of passages in the New Testament insist on making Jesus into tyrant king who will rule over the entire cosmos and demand servanthood from his followers. And neither the medieval nor the modern Christian Church has done much to implement Jesus' reversal of hierarchies.

Early Christians Challenged to Let Go of their Boundaries

When we look at the actions and letters of the Apostles, we encounter the struggle of the early Church with the issue of exclusivity and the relation of insiders to outsiders. Surprisingly enough there seems to have been little or no disagreement among the first group of Christians, who were all Jews, about the inclusion of Samaritans as followers of Jesus Christ. Chapter Eight of the book of Acts records their incorporation into the Church community as transcending racial and theological barriers.

It was quite a different story, however, when it came to the idea of accepting other gentiles as recipients of God's grace in Christ. The early chapters of Acts portray the first Christian community as a widely diverse group of believers, but they were nonetheless all Jews. It can be argued that the central drama of the early Church was the issue of Gentile believers, a drama that was set in motion by Paul's journeys to the regions outside of Palestine where he preached the Gospel to Jews and Gentiles alike. There were those who insisted that if these non-Jewish believers were to become true Christians they would need to submit to being circumcised, to becoming good Jews before becoming Christians.

This controversy was brought to a head at the first Jerusalem Council where both sides of the issue were set forth and a decision was reached to break down the barrier between Jewish and Gentile believers. The Fifteenth Chapter of Acts records this dramatic and absolutely crucial development. Peter testified that God "made no distinction between us and them," and James concluded that no one should impose any "irksome restrictions on those of the Gentiles who are turning to God."

In his letter to the Christians in Galatia, Paul addressed this issue directly and focused his own convictions, as well as a pivotal New Testament emphasis, in these words: "In Christ there is no such thing as Jew or Greek, slave or free, male or female. We are all one in Christ." [Galatians 3:28]

Unfortunately, the early Church had great difficulty learning to embody such inclusive truth. In this same passage in Galatians, for instance, Peter is said to have been reprimanded by Paul for choosing not to eat with Gentiles at a gathering of believers in Antioch. Paul was upset with Peter for this inconsistency. Moreover, Paul was often hounded by Jewish Christians who refused to abide by the decision of the Jerusalem Council. These "Judaizers" went to the cities where Paul had established small congregations and tried to get new Christians to submit to circumcision.

In his letter to the Galatian Christians, Paul wastes no time in pointing out the error of their ways. It seems, however, that even Paul himself struggled with how to put the inclusiveness of the Gospel to work in the practical life of faith. For one thing, he had nothing directly to say about the practice of slavery being wrong. Even though in his letter to his friend Philemon he urges him to accept his runaway slave Onesimus—who had recently become a believer—as a "brother in Christ," it is unclear whether Paul meant that Philemon should set Onesimus free or simply treat him with Christian respect. This issue did not receive resolution in the early Church until several centuries later. And as we know, the issue of slavery has had to be readdressed at various times by Christians and others all over the world, even now in our own time.

Paul also had some difficulty on another aspect of inclusiveness. It is evident in his letters that women played an important, even crucial, role in carrying out the ministry he began. Paul explicitly names several women as his "co-workers in Christ" in a number of his salutations [Romans 16, I Corinthians 16, and II Timothy 4:19], and both Lydia [Acts 16] and Phoebe [Romans 16] clearly played a key part in the functioning of these beginning congregations. Yet there are several other passages in these letters where Paul clearly abides by the traditional view that women should take a subservient position to men in both church and home life. [I. Corinthians 14: 34-45] It is not easy to reconcile these two perspectives in Paul's writings, though some scholars have attempted to do so.

Throughout all this we are once again confronted with the question of outsiders and insiders within the Christian community. The cultural and doctrinal borders in place when the early Church was born defined its context and struggles, just as our own cultural norms and prejudices define the context and struggles of the Church today. Throughout history, humans have always drawn together in such a fashion as to exclude others who are different in some way. But the Gospel of Christ is aimed directly at overcoming this kind of destructive exclusion that debilitates the integrity of the insiders even as it harms the outsiders. Borders and barriers that serve as a way to exclude and denigrate other persons must be crossed and eventually dissolved. This is a never ending task for such boundaries continuously resurrect themselves.

There are at least two additional aspects of Borderland Theology that should be taken up at this juncture. The first has to do with experience of Pentecost in the formation of the first Christian community in Jerusalem, while the second pertains to the conversion of Saul of Tarsus to Paul the Apostle.

On the day of Pentecost the Apostles were startled by what sounded like a mighty wind and what looked like tongues of fire over each individual's head. Then "they were all filled with the Holy Spirit and began to talk in other tongues, as the Spirit gave them utterance." [Acts 2:4]

The tongues in question here were the specific natural languages of the various Jewish people who happened to be in Jerusalem at the time. These people were astounded to hear members of this group of Galileans speaking to them in their own tongue about the life, death, and resurrection of Jesus. With respect to our theme of insiders and outsiders, the significance of this event lies in the power of God's Spirit to enable believers to stretch across customary boundaries and barriers to communicate the good news of God's inclusive love. The images of flaming tongues symbolized the overcoming of those cultural limitations that separate different peoples from one another and from God. In this episode the idea of Borderland Theology becomes especially relevant because many people from different countries were brought together by the communicative efforts of these early believers.

The story of the conversion of Paul is another instance of transforming an outsider into an insider and all of the difficulties that entails. [Acts 9] Saul of Tarsus had been one of the chief Jewish persecutors of the initial group of Christians. He had witnessed the stoning of Stephen and had set out for Damascus to round up any Jews who had become Christians and bring them to trial in Jerusalem. From Saul's standpoint, Christians were outsiders while from their standpoint he himself was an outsider. The whole story is intensified by the fact that Saul was from a city that lay outside of Palestine, one strongly influenced by Greco-Roman culture.

After Saul became a Christian and took the name Paul, the Christians in Damascus were highly suspicious of this outsider who was now claiming to be one of them. Even though Ananias had been given a vision in which he was told to receive Saul into their community, it took three years for the community to fully accept him. The dynamics of such transformation are important because crossing borders like the ones that existed between Jews and Christians at this early stage of the Church's development was by no means a trivial matter. Paul himself surely had a number of serious issues that had to be resolved in his own life and thought as he worked his way into the

Christian community. Moreover, those believers already committed to "the way," as it was called, must have found it very difficult to overlook the previous persecution perpetrated by Saul and receive him as Paul. Fortunately, he was able to prove the sincerity of his new-found faith.

One of the more interesting and instructive features of Paul's transformation from outsider to insider is his continuing effort to connect the new Gospel of inclusiveness in Christ with his traditional Jewish faith. For Paul did not simply put his former religious beliefs aside when he became a Christian. Rather, he, like most of the early Jewish believers, saw his new-found faith as the fulfillment of his traditional religion. Thus in his writings he frequently sought to explain just how these two forms of faith are to be understood as connected. Chapters nine through eleven of his letter to the Christians in Rome is an excellent example of this effort, for there he introduces the image of grafting new branches onto a tree as a way of explaining the relation between these two faiths.

In the process of crossing and transforming borders, then, it is not always necessary, let alone desirable, to set one point of view aside in order to participate in another. It is sometimes possible to incorporate different points of view and traditions into each other so as to create a richer, more comprehensive perspective. Also, not all borders and distinctions need to be overcome, for some may serve a useful purpose, like keeping invaders at bay or protecting people from being harmed by vicious criminals. Nevertheless, the inclusiveness of the Gospel requires that all barriers that exclude and oppress some persons to the benefit of others need to be destroyed and transformed.

The power as well as the difficulty of the struggle that may be involved in such transformation is aptly depicted in the following story of how Peter came to see that even one's enemy, a Roman soldier, can and must be included in the Gospel. [Acts 10] We are told at the outset of the chapter that a Roman centurion named Cornelius, who "was a religious man and he and his whole family joined in the worship of God," received a vision in which he was instructed to locate a person named Simon Peter. So Cornelius sent his servant to find Peter.

The Christian Scriptures 51

About the same time Peter was on a rooftop waiting for his lunch to be prepared when he fell into a trance. He saw a sheet being let down from the sky, full of every sort of creature, and he heard a voice saying, "Up, Peter, kill and eat." Peter refused the command protesting that he had never eaten anything that was unclean and was not about to start now. It is significant to note that Peter clearly recognized the voice as that of God, for he addressed his response to the "Lord." So here was Peter once again talking back to God even as he had done innumerable times during his years with Jesus.

The sheet and the command to eat of the animals in it was offered to Peter three times, but each time he refused. Each time he was told, "It is not for you to call profane what God counts as clean." At about this time the messengers from Cornelius showed up at the front door asking for Peter. Cornelius was a Roman Gentile who would have had very different ideas of what foods were to be eaten and what foods were to be considered unclean. After puzzling over the meaning of all this, Peter became convinced that he should be hospitable to these men and go with them to Cornelius' house. The result was that Peter had opportunity to share the Gospel with Cornelius' household.

What is especially interesting about this episode are the dynamics of Peter's decision to rearrange his categories concerning insiders and outsiders. Here is a classic case of an established boundary between two groups of people—the Jews and Roman Gentiles—being dissolved by the energy of God's Spirit.

It is crucial to understand the depth of Peter's struggle and its far-reaching consequences for the Christian Church. Peter's way of expressing his own transformation was in terms of the notion that God does not play favorites, but rather seeks those who sincerely seek to "worship in spirit and in truth." This was an amazing revelation to Peter, as well as to most other Jewish believers, and it led to the radical idea that all people, no matter what their background, culture, race, or religion, can be included within the Christian community.

The Radical Nature of God's Inclusion

From our present day vantage point it is easy for us to fail to appreciate the radical character of this event. Here was the Jewish religion being opened up to include those whom it had traditionally excluded because God was now understood as an all-embracing power of love and grace. We need only look around at various versions of the contemporary Christian Church to find corners where this truth has not yet found its way. Christians regularly exclude certain people, whether on purpose or inadvertently, because they do not dress properly, vote correctly, earn enough money, or have the same skin color, social background, or sexual orientation.

Peter's vision thrust itself upon him from the outside; it was a kind of "burning bush" experience in which he was startled into recognition of the presence of God. Moreover, it directly attacked one of the most cherished of Jewish beliefs, namely that they as a chosen people were special and closer to God than all other peoples. Indeed, as we have seen, the Jews of Jesus' day looked upon all non-Jews as "dogs."

What these Hebrews had forgotten, however, was that when God called them out to be an especially blessed people they were also told that they would be a blessing to all nations. They were not to think of themselves as an end in itself, but as a means to the enrichment of all the people of the earth. The sort of radical inclusiveness exemplified in the life and death of Jesus constituted a head-on challenge to the elitism that had characterized the Jewish nation, including those who had now become Christians. Peter was here beginning to grasp this astounding truth.

What we see in Peter's struggle, then, is precisely what Paul was talking about in the first verses of chapter twelve of his letter to the Roman Christians: "Be not conformed to this world, but be transformed by the renewing of your mind that you might prove what is the good and acceptable will of God." Such a turnaround represents nothing short of a conversion.

An extremely powerful example of the depth of this type of conversion experience is found in Will Campbell's extraordinary book, *Brother to a Dragonfly*. In it he relates how he, after serving many years as a Christian minister, came to understand the true meaning of the Gospel of Christ. Two of his civil rights advocate friends had been murdered by some Klansmen in Mississippi and he was wrestling with how to reconcile this tragedy with his belief in God's love. One of his friends, who had never been a believer, challenged him to summarize the Gospel in 25 words or less.

After some thought, Will gave his answer: "We're all bastards, but God loves us anyway." Then his friend asked if God loved the two friends who had been murdered. Will answered that of course God did. "What about the rednecks who murdered them? Does God love them too?" All at once Will became silent. He went to the window and stared out at the night. It was then that he realized the startling truth of the Gospel, and dates his real Christian conversion from that very moment. God loves even redneck murderers. From that point on Will Campbell began to meet with Klan members as well as go to civil rights meetings in an effort to embody reconciliation, and a bit later on somebody burned a cross on his front lawn.

It was this deep sense of God's all inclusive love and grace that Peter experienced on the rooftop in Jerusalem that day when he decided to go to the house of Cornelius. God loves those whom we hate, as well as those who hate us—and God!! This is the kind of being we see God to be in the person of Jesus Christ, one who dares to cross borders of tradition and hate, to risk misunderstanding, suffering, and even death in order to bring about reconciliation.

The God of Judgment or Compassion?

All of this brings us to a final and more complex theme running through the Christian Scriptures. Throughout both the Gospel accounts of Jesus' life and Paul's letters to young churches there seems to be a conflict between the emphasis on the all-encompassing love of God and the notion of a final judgment in which this same God is depicted as vindictively sentencing nonbelievers to hell. In spite of the stress upon the grace and forgiveness of God in the work of reconciliation provided by Christ, there are a number of passages in the New Testament in which we are told that God will conquer and destroy evil and punish those who have participated in it.

Indeed, Philippians Chapter Two, which focuses the self-sacrificing love and servanthood of Christ as a cosmic border-crosser, is followed immediately by a passage that portrays Christ as an all-powerful potentate before whom all persons will prostrate themselves. The Gospels also contain accounts of how the Son of Humanity will come in power to reward the righteous and punish the wicked. I find the tension between these two different images of God both puzzling and very disturbing because the former stresses God's willingness to set aside the very prerogatives which the latter extols.

Some attempt to gloss over this tension by various theological shuffles which generally tend to beg the very question at issue, namely does God love humanity because Christ came or did Christ come because God loves humanity? In the first instance we have an angry God who was appeased by Christ's life and work while in the second we have the God who loved us "while we were yet sinners." It seems clear that the one precludes the other.

For the purposes of this chapter the crucial concern here is how these conflicting images of God and Christ relate to the question of insiders versus outsiders. For clearly, the notion of a final judgment in which some are rewarded and others are punished strongly suggests an ultimate classification people into these two categories. The difficulty is that this idea flatly contradicts the main theme of the Gospel, namely that God forgives and accepts everyone, even though some refuse to accept God's grace in return.

Nowhere does this portrayal of God as a vindictive being come across more forcefully than in the book of Revelation. In spite of the emphasis throughout this apocalyptic vision on the Lamb of God, there are numerous passages where God almost gleefully divides "the sheep from the goats," sending the latter to eternal damnation. In line with this sort of royal judgment theme are those passages where God is said to finally conquer and destroy all the powers of evil in the world in order to create a new heaven and a new earth. Thus God's victory is said to depend upon force rather than on love and persuasion.

It is frequently claimed that this tension is only apparent, since God is a just ruler and in the end is free to deal with sinners and evil as a righteous judge or sovereign king. But this surely flies in the face of the other New Testament focus, which I take to be more central to the core of the Christian Gospel, that out of divine love God has chosen to serve as the suffering servant of humankind by seeking to overcome all barriers and borders, both those between persons and those between persons and God.

My own view of how these two conflicting images of God and Christ came to exist side by side in the Christian Bible is that those who were responsible for the writing of the New Testament, even as the disciples in the Gospel stories, were frequently unable to accept the radical character of God as revealed in the person of Jesus Christ. The idea that God is not really a heavenly king, a sovereign judge, but a humble and loving servant or parent, was simply too much for them to take in. Although Jesus continually presented himself and God as such, his followers did not feel comfortable with this way of thinking about Divine Reality and preferred to keep God on a heavenly throne, ruling over the world and its citizens.

As I see it, the God revealed in Jesus Christ was and is no more interested in "lording it over" creation than a loving parent would be in relation to a child. In crossing the border in order to reconcile humans to one another and to Divine Reality, God set aside all the hierarchical barriers generally associated with kings and ownership so as to become the "friend" [John 15] and "elder brother" [Hebrews 11] of whoever would receive such grace.

Another way to put this point is to say that Christ's true glory and exaltation are not to be found in an ability to reign and rule as a cosmic king, but in the capacity to bear the burdens and sins of humankind. If this is not the case, then the entire Incarnation turns out to be a mere charade in which God only pretends to become one of us. I believe the very concept of "triumph" as depicted in Revelation needs to be defined in light of the Incarnation rather than the other way around.

Finally, then, what about the ultimate conquest of evil? Here again the frequent picture is that of God exercising all cosmic power in order to destroy everything that stands in the way of the divine plan, including "the world, the flesh, and the devil." God is often portrayed as vanquishing evil by the sheer force of superiority, crushing the opposition and punishing its perpetrators. Then, as John puts it in his visionary Revelation, everyone shall be given their just due in accordance with the quality of their earthly life and all shall know that Christ is "King of kings and Lord of lords." [Revelation 19:16]

I believe, however, that the ultimate power of God lies in redemptive love rather than in cosmic force. The victory of the Divine Reality over the forces of evil through the power of acceptance and persuasion, and through unconditional love, is far more in harmony with the Gospel of reconciliation as seen in the life and person of Jesus Christ than is that of sheer conquest and destruction. God's love in Christ will somehow incorporate rather than annihilate those forces that oppose it.

Just as the opposing force of gravity can be creatively incorporated into the building of an arch as the individual stones are stacked upon one another, so the forces of evil and destruction will be integrated into God's ultimate act of reconciliation. In the end, an arch is held together by the placing of the keystone at its apex, even as Christ "holds all things together" [Col. 1:17] by embracing rather than rejecting opposing forces.

In the Incarnation God chose to bridge the gaps created by human-made barriers between insiders and outsiders, haves and have-nots, "sinners" and "saints," and especially the barriers that separate humanity from Divine Grace and Love.

Part Two

The Church and

Borderlands

4

The Church In World History

Conquering and Dividing

When we turn to the history of the Christian Church, the issues clustering around the relationship between insiders and outsiders do not fade away. In fact, if anything they intensify. This chapter will sketch the history of the Church to show that in spite of the Gospel's call to do away with the borders and barriers that separate people from one another, Christians have frequently failed to integrate the insight and power of this message into their corporate life.

Even in their own homeland, Christian believers began as outsiders within the context of the Roman Empire. They were also outsiders from the perspective of orthodox Jews. In the early centuries of this era the Roman authorities systematically persecuted those who professed Christ as their Lord and God. In spite of this—or as some have maintained, because of it—the number of those who became Christians steadily increased. The Gospel spread throughout the Empire and found a home in the hearts of many thousands of people.

Constantine Makes Christianity a State Religion

The turning point that reversed this insider-outsider pattern was the conversion of the Emperor Constantine around 322 A.D. Constantine claimed to have seen a vision of the cross of Christ and to have heard a voice proclaiming, "In this sign conquer." Once embraced by Constantine, Christianity became the official State religion and was transformed from a faith of persecuted outsiders into one of insiders.

Although this transformation did not come to pass overnight, it was not long before Constantine exerted strong leadership in matters of faith as well as in matters of state. He instituted influential Church councils and relocated the center of his empire from Rome to Byzantium at the place where Europe and the Middle East meet. He did this in order to place the capital of what later came to be called the "Holy Roman Empire" further to the East so as to unite the Latin and Greek regions of the faithful. He even renamed the city after himself, Constantinople.

After his death, those in power returned the capital of the Empire to Rome and the Church continued to prosper within the structure provided by such political protection. Soon it even began to pattern its own organizational structure after that of the Empire, with bishops in each of the major cities and the chief bishop in Rome. Eventually, however, the Empire crumbled and the Church was forced to redefine its role in relation to the ensuing political power struggles of the Mediterranean area.

Some contend that the conversion of Constantine and the adoption of the Empire's hierarchical chain of command were the two worst things that could ever have happened to the Christian church, since they amounted to its full captivation by the powers of secular society and led to its nearly total contamination. The Kingdom of Christ became a worldly kingdom which down through the centuries has been characterized by corruption and imperialism.

The Coptic Community is Marginalized

Before the Church became fully unified under Roman rule the first major division between insiders and outsiders took place. This division was between the Roman or Latin contingent and the Coptic Christian community in Egypt, which thrived between 200 and 600 A.D. Our knowledge of this division is the result of the mid 1940s discovery of an entire library of writings compiled by the Coptic Christians and preserved in an area known as Nag Hammadi.

It has become apparent that the result of the struggle between these two factions within the Church was the subjugation and essential disappearance of the Coptic community from the story of Christianity. The Roman and Greek faction became the dominant group of insiders while the Coptic community was relegated to the fringes, becoming outsiders in relation to power structure of the Church. The inclusive character of the Christian Gospel was not able to overcome this conflict.

The Nag Hammadi texts, especially the Gospel of Thomas, appear to be the expression of a quite different understanding of the Christian Gospel dating from very early in the Church's history. Most of the texts seem to expound a very mystical view of the relation between Jesus and God and between Jesus and his disciples, one that involves a special sort of insiders' secret knowledge. This has led scholars to designate this perspective on Christian faith as a "Gnostic Gospel" (from a Greek word for knowledge), associating it with those interpretations of the Gospel that claimed to have a unique key to understanding the message of Jesus.

Since all versions of Gnosticism were deemed heretical by the orthodox branch of the Church, which eventually became the "official" version, the Nag Hammadi writings probably represent the point of view of a group of Christians who were in one way or another eliminated from the main stream of Christian history. It is ironic that such believers, who claimed to have an insiders' true understanding of the faith, would eventually become outsiders in relation to the dominant forces controlling the development of the Church at large.

In general, modern Christians know very little about the power struggles that took place within the Church down through its long history, especially those that transpired in the very early centuries. Numerous Church Councils decided, after much heated debate, what the "true" church would really believe, and those that disagreed were forced out of the community. Although this process is in many ways quite understandable, it does raise serious questions concerning the insider-outsider issue in relation to the Christian Gospel.

Divisions between Roman Catholic and Orthodox Churches

After Constantine's death the church in Rome once again exerted itself and became for all practical purposes the official center of Christendom. Over the ensuing centuries a serious rift arose between this Western version of Christianity, which adopted Latin as the standard means of expressing the Gospel and Christian teaching, and that which continued to follow the Eastern version centered in Constantinople and using Greek as its official language. The disagreement finally came to a head around the year 1000 A.D. when the Roman bishop had a pronouncement of excommunication delivered to the church leaders in Constantinople. The Eastern Church leaders reciprocated in kind.

One of the major sources of conflict between these two perspectives on the Christian Church was precisely the role to be played by the bishops of various cities and provinces throughout the world. The leaders in the West believed that Rome should be the only center and head of the church, while those in the East, primarily in Russia and Greece, continued to hold out for a more democratic version of church leadership shared by all leaders. Those in the East also insisted on Greek as the official language of the Church since the New Testament was written in this language.

Another point of contention in this struggle was what to us today might seem trivial, namely a doctrinal question about the relationship between the Holy Spirit and Christ. The Roman Church affirmed that the Holy Spirit "flows from" (*filioque* in Latin) Jesus Christ (the Son) and is thus subordinate to the Son. The Eastern church, on the other hand, was adamant that these two persons of the trinity are equals in relation to God the Father.

Once again we are confronted with the question of insiders and outsiders. The Western branch of Christendom came to be known as the Roman Catholic Church and the Eastern branch calls itself the Orthodox Church. Each has consistently viewed the other as basically heretical or schismatic, and there has been virtually no cooperation between them over the past ten centuries. While the Roman Church has spread throughout the world, the Orthodox Church remains pretty much limited to Russia, some of the Baltic countries, Greece, and Ethiopia.

Within both of these branches of the Church there are a number of divisions that are also various versions of the insider-outsider conflict. Over the years of the American experience, a strong tension has developed between those Catholics who seek to embody a more progressive expression of the Faith and those who remain loyal to the Roman tradition. This is especially evident in many Latin American countries where Liberation Theology has arisen in response to the political and economic oppression of the peasant population. There are also serious tensions among Catholics in various parts of Europe and Africa.

The Orthodox Church, too, occasionally exhibits internal conflicts, since each Patriarchate is essentially autonomous. When the brilliant Greek writer Nikos Kazantzakis died, for instance, the Bishop of Athens refused to let him be buried on the mainland because he deemed him a heretic. The Bishop of Crete, who is under a different Patriarchate, however, allowed him to be buried there, since next to El Greco, Kazantzakis is the island's most famous son.

There are other differences between the Roman and Orthodox Churches as well. In the Catholic Church rationalist and mystical emphases are equally strong, but in Orthodoxy mysticism clearly dominates. Also, as a result of the Second Vatican Council held in 1963-65, the church service is now conducted in the local language rather than in Latin. In addition, Catholic priests now face the congregation, rather than facing the altar. In Orthodoxy, the worship service is almost always in Greek and the altar remains out of the view behind a screen where only the priest may go.

In all of the above cases it is easy to see the reality of the insider-outsider motif operative throughout the entire church, from the Middle Ages right down to the present. The scenario is almost always the same. One faction concludes that its understanding of the Gospel and its particular practices are the only true ones, and all other versions are deemed to be heretical or schismatic. The insiders place themselves over and against, if not above, the outsiders, and often serious conflicts cause deep wounds and irreparable damage.

It is as pathetic as it is debilitating to reflect on this phenomenon as it displays itself throughout the life of the Church. In the 17th chapter of John's Gospel, Jesus prays that all his followers would be united in love, and the first Epistle of John states that the world shall be amazed at "how these Christians love each other." As the well-known song has it, "They'll know we are Christians by our love." To a great extent these sentiments still remain unfulfilled.

The Protestant Reformation

The next major division within the history of the Church was the Protestant Reformation, which emerged as the result of Martin Luther nailing his "95 Theses" to the door of the cathedral in Wittenburg, Germany. What began as a conflict in the soul of a single monk over the basis of faith developed into an all-out struggle between the religious and political forces that wanted to reform if not overthrow the Catholic Church, and those that sought to retain the hegemony Rome had established down through the many centuries of Christendom.

The focal point of the Reformation was the doctrine of salvation. Luther and his followers were of the opinion that the way the Church was operating led people to believe that salvation in Christ depended on the individual believer's performance of certain penitential rituals and works, rather than on the grace of God alone through faith. The way Luther read the writings of Paul made it clear to him that this interpretation of the Gospel was wrong, and he set about to reform the Church accordingly. It never occurred to Luther that he was about to cause a watershed division within the Christian Church itself.

At issue in this struggle was not just the doctrine of salvation, but the whole question of the nature of ecclesiastical authority. The Catholic Church viewed the word of the Pope as an ultimate source of authority, since he spoke for the Christian community itself. Luther maintained that the Pope obtained his authority from the scripture, while the Catholic Church argued that the scripture got its authority from the Church, since the Church produced, transmitted, and interpreted the Bible.

This question of authority has remained a crucial one ever since. Protestants have adopted the scripture as the one final authority for "Faith and Life," while Catholics continue to maintain that the Vatican is the final authority. In its argument against Luther at the time of his trial, the Vatican in essence said that if the Church allowed individual and/or groups of believers to decide for themselves what the scriptures teach, the Church would become hopelessly divided into numerous splintered communities.

History has, of course, proven this prediction to be correct, since we cannot even count the number of factions of the Christian Church in the world today. Nearly every group has subdivided itself into many versions; there are, for example, at least six kinds of Presbyterians, five kinds of Lutherans, and who knows how many kinds of Baptists in the United States alone. Someone once counted over two hundred different religious groups listed in the Los Angeles yellow pages. We have come to take this state of affairs for granted, but it casts a dark shadow over the Christian Gospel and its claim to reveal reconciling truth to humankind.

So here again we encounter the insider-outsider reality. Catholics have continued to count Protestants as outsiders and Protestants do likewise with Catholics. Many wars and heresy trials have been conducted in the name of the Church, and Protestants themselves have behaved disgracefully toward one another in the name of "the truth." Even today in Ireland, the former Yugoslavia, and other countries, Christians still kill each other and people of other faiths as well.

The 20th Century: The Liberal and Conservative Church

Another drawing of boundaries and setting up of borders in the Church arose at the turn of the 20th Century between liberals and conservatives. As a result of the emergence of what is called the "modern mind," developing out of the Enlightenment and the rise of science, religious thinkers and theologians of the late 19th Century began to question many of the traditional doctrines of the Christian Faith and especially the authority of the Bible. In brief, they took a more liberal approach to religious issues from the standard orthodoxy of previous centuries.

The focal point of the conservative reaction to this sort of liberalism was the publication in 1905 of a series of small paperback books called *The Fundamentals* sponsored by a group of teachers and pastors from both the United States and Great Britain. "Fundamentalism" gets its name from this set of books. About half way through the 20th century a number of conservative scholars began to separate themselves out from the fundamentalists, preferring to call themselves "evangelicals." These thinkers were far more willing to engage in dialogue with their more liberal Christian colleagues and to re-examine certain traditional doctrinal points.

This split between liberals and fundamentalists was somewhat softened by the rise in mid-century of what came to be known as "Neo-Orthodox" theology. In this case it was a number of more liberal thinkers, such as Reinhold Niebuhr and Karl Barth, who began to swing back toward traditional doctrines like original sin and the need for grace. By the end of the 20th century, Evangelicalism and Neo-orthodoxy had almost become synonymous.

As is well known, one of the major debates in this controversy between liberals and conservatives revolved around the theory of evolution. Darwin's ideas concerning natural selection as the explanation of the emergence of human life from previous and less complex animal life seemed to fly in the face of the Judeo-Christian belief in God's creation of both the world and human beings. The famous Scopes Trial in Tennessee served to focus the emotions, if not the issues, surrounding this conflict.

Often this debate boils down to different understandings of the nature of the Judeo-Christian scriptures. Conservatives generally seek to take the Bible literally, in the sense that it must be considered to be accurate in all scientific matters and without error of any kind. Those of a more liberal view see scripture as composed of a variety of kinds of literature from history and story to poetry and myth (in the rich rather than the trivial sense). Thus the latter see no need for the Bible to be scientifically accurate to be authoritative in matters of Christian faith and practice.

The history of the Christian Church, then, is the story of one group after another setting up barriers and borders that have divided believers from each other and from various groups of non-believers. This hardly seems consistent with the major thrust of the Christian message, that "God was in Christ reconciling the world." As the New Testament has it, God came into the world in the person of Jesus Christ, itself a border crossing act, in order to overcome the borders that we humans erect as defensive and evasive strategies.

We can say that such divisions and borders have always existed among humans, that it is only "natural" for there to be insiders and outsiders. To some extent this is surely true, for we must never forget that even when we carry divine grace in the life of the Christian community we do so in "earthen vessels." Thus our various embodiments of the Incarnational Gospel will always fall short of the goals for which God intends them. Nonetheless, the number and degree of the divisions between and among Christians is at best disappointing and at worst downright appalling.

Ecumenism: Reconciliation in the Christian Church

Fortunately, not all of the Christian story reads like a tag-team wrestling match. Here and there over the centuries there have been occasions for cooperation and even unification. Much of the progress made in this direction has taken place in the 20th century, specifically in the decades since World War II. It is time to turn to these developments to attempt to balance out the record.

The spread of Christianity around the world, beginning with the modern missionary movement in the 19th century and continuing on throughout the 20th century, in spite of two world wars, eventually contributed to a gradual trend toward unification within the Church. Once the Gospel had spread to nearly every continent and country in the world there was a tendency toward interconnection that slowly wove a fabric of commonality among all of the various outposts and resulting versions of the faith. This happened in both the Catholic Church and Protestant denominations.

The great diversity that had come to characterize Protestantism began to give way to a spirit of cooperation and merging that had not been seen in the Church since its inception. The lack of central control among Protestant churches had initially led to a great deal of competition and name-calling between the different versions of the faith around the world. Now this divisiveness began to dissolve, perhaps at least partially because of the need to work together in the context of the political struggles in Europe. The new efforts of various factions of the Christian Church to put aside their differences and work together was called Ecumenism.

The monolithic structures of the Roman Catholic Church and the Eastern Orthodox Church, however, have not altered much, and these two ecclesiastical bodies continue to remain somewhat aloof from the ecumenical movement. But there have been some significant changes in the Catholic Church. For instance, the Roman Catholic Church does now dialogue with the World Council of Churches, and has joined with the Lutheran Churches in affirming that Martin Luther was right in insisting that salvation is by grace and faith alone. In addition, there are a myriad of ecumenical efforts at the local levels that join Catholics and Protestants in work toward common goals.

The World Council of Churches and Ecumenical Bodies

As the world began to shrink by virtue of the technological revolution and as indigenous leadership began to emerge in newly independent non-Western nations, believers were brought closer together in their effort to live out their faith. A great number of Christian clergy and lay people began to feel deep embarrassment over the divisions that had come to characterize the Christian Church. It was time to demonstrate to the rest of the world the "oneness of believers in Christ."

This desire for unity in Christ expressed itself in 1948 with the formation of the World Council of Churches with members all around the globe. By 1952 the membership in this organization had risen to 158 different churches in 43 countries. Throughout the world many groups sought ways to cooperate with one another, while others actually joined in official mergers and unifications that wiped away their differences. Still others founded associations and federations in order to bring their respective organizations closer to one another.

This trend toward Christian unity and love kept apace right down to the close of the 20th century, though it did begin to wane in the latter decades. Many different denominations, such as the largest branches of Presbyterianism in the United States, the Presbyterian Church U.S.A. (in the north) and the United Presbyterian Church (in the south), joined in a merger. Also some Lutheran churches have joined together, as have a number of Baptists, Methodists, and Congregationalists. Many of these groups have even cosponsored conferences and church councils.

National counterparts to the World Council of Churches also arose in many individual countries. In the United States, the National Council of Churches has for several decades provided leadership for the drive toward Christian unity, while in Great Britain and various other countries of Europe similar national bodies have been very active. Indeed, in Europe a broader cross-section of believers has been achieved than in the United States where Catholics, Evangelicals, and Pentecostals have chosen to remain outside of the ecumenical movement.

Unfortunately, here in the United States, the National Council of Churches has been moving slowly toward financial bankruptcy.

The Church in World History

Its struggle to maintain itself greatly diminishes its ability to function effectively to fulfill its stated goals. The National Council of Churches has recently appointed new leadership and overhauled its financial structure, however, thus giving promise for a more vital future, though the refusal of the Catholic Church and of most conservative Protestant organizations to participate in the Council continues to frustrate its overall goal.

There are those who are unsurprised by these developments since they are of the conviction that no real progress in the world ever comes from organizational hierarchies, filtering down to the grassroots of the Church from the top. They hold that all revolutionary movements must come from below, and that the desire for Christian unity is no exception to this pattern. Perhaps the future yet holds a more viable form of unity.

Joint Declaration by Catholics and Lutherans

As a specific and significant case in point with regard to the movement toward Christian unity, we should consider recent events in the relationship between the Roman Catholic Church and the Lutheran World Federation which took place in Germany. Early in the 1990s the Catholic Church issued a statement to the effect that Martin Luther had been right in his interpretation of Paul's writings regarding the basis of faith being grace rather than works. This surely was an historical landmark in the history of Christianity and one that set the stage for the event taking place on October 31, 1999, exactly 482 years to the day after Luther had nailed his 95 theses to the church door in Wittenburg, Germany.

In St. Anna's Lutheran Church in Augsburg, Germany at precisely 11:20 am, Cardinal Edward Cassidy, President of the Vatican's Pontifical Council for Promoting Christian Unity and Lutheran Bishop Christian Krause signed the Joint Declaration on the Doctrine of Justification. According to this document there is now a consensus in basic truths between Lutherans and Catholics on the doctrine of justification by faith alone rather than works. The avowed goal of this far-reaching agreement is to put an end to the enmity that has existed between these two Church bodies for over 400 years.

Although this agreement in no way brings the two groups of believers closer together at the political level, let alone the ritualistic level, it does signal a sign of fresh hope in the ongoing effort toward greater Church unity. Both the Catholic and Lutheran leadership have indicated that much is still needed to bring these branches of Christendom together, but they have indicated their intention of pursuing this goal.

Here again we see how the borders and barriers between various branches of the Christian Church that have been separated from one another for centuries can be transcended. A Borderland Theology view of the Christian faith is clear in saying that the Incarnation requires that such borders be both crossed and eventually eliminated. In Christ, God bridged the chasm between divinity and humanity, and modeled how we in turn should bridge those chasms that separate people from one another, especially when they claim to worship the same God and believe the same Gospel. This is the true meaning of Border Theology.

Divisions between Christianity and Other Religions

The puzzling and at the same time deeply discouraging thing about all the divisions in the Christian Church is that most if not all of these barriers and boundaries were initially set up in order to purify and protect the Gospel of Jesus Christ. In fact, however, they have resulted in great distortions and contradictions of that very Gospel.

One only needs to return to the notion of the Incarnation and to Paul's summary statement of it, "God was in Christ reconciling the world. . ." in order to see that any and all attempts to protect and purify the Gospel by excluding those who disagree with our own understanding of it are doomed from the outset. To raise a standard next to the reconciling cross of Christ and to call on people to rally around it is one thing, but to begin by excluding those who propose a different understanding of that cross is to contradict its meaning.

This is not to say that any and every interpretation of the Incarnation must be accepted, since this posture would surely produce as much chaos and division as has been seen in the more sectarian history of the Church. Nevertheless the spirit and energy of an inclusive posture is quite different from that of an exclusive one, and it is the former that is entailed by the Gospel of Incarnation. As we have seen, the Biblical story, especially that of the New Testament, makes this very clear.

All the foregoing examples speak only of theological borders within the Christian Church itself. But I should also mention borders and resulting conflicts that have arisen between Christians and people of other faiths altogether. Once it was decided that the Christian Faith was the "One True Faith," it was only a short step to the conclusion that people of other religions were not only lost, but were potential enemies of the church as well.

This attitude of superiority led the official Christian church to perpetrate untold attacks and acts of oppression on people who held alternative beliefs. The virtual merging of the Christian Church with the Roman Empire, and later with medieval rulers, brought with it a combination of arrogance and power that resulted in numerous hostilities and wars between Christians and people of other faiths.

The more outstanding examples of Christian aggression include the destruction of the great library at Alexandria, the crusades against the Islamic people dwelling in Jerusalem, the persecution of Jews from the Middle Ages right on up to the Holocaust in Germany, and even the modern conquest of Africa, India, and the Americas. In addition to racism and a quest for power, all of these conflicts were fed by a sense of exclusive and arrogant religious zeal. It is, of course, true that Christians were not the only ones instigating these conflicts. Other religions have often established borders of their own.

Towards an Understanding with Those of Other Faiths

If we were to chart the various possible attitudes toward other religions along a continuum, with a "We have the entire Truth" attitude on one extreme and a "There is no Truth" attitude on the other, Christianity—along with most other religions—would be closest to the end of the spectrum that believes that it has the entire Truth. Groups on this end of the spectrum come to some interpretation of the Truth and then do not allow other interpretations.

At the opposite extreme is the modern view that truth is strictly a function of one's cultural or personal point of view or perspective. All claims to beliefs and knowledge are relative to the persons affirming them, and therefore there is no such thing as "Truth" with a capital "T." This approach equates truth with the angle from which one views it. Some say, however, that the problem with this idea is that it leads to skepticism and that it nullifies all beliefs including its own claim to truth.

In my opinion, a more helpful approach stands at the center of the continuum. Here one acknowledges that one's individual and/or cultural perspectives do in fact shape the nature of Truth, but at the same time also affirms that there exists a common truth at which we all aim as we engage in our various searches for knowledge. In this approach there is a place both for humility and confidence as we enter into dialogue together. Through mutual openness and discussion, this posture seeks to overcome the barriers and borders that result from the ethnocentric perspectives that are a natural outgrowth of specific historical and cultural contexts.

As we have seen, the Christian Church for the most part has not, at least until recent decades, tried to follow this middle way. Rather, Christians have assumed an exclusive hold on the Truth in matters of religion and have behaved in a condescending manner at best, and in an oppressive manner at worst, toward those of other faiths. Hindus, Buddhists, Jews, and Native Peoples alike have all suffered severely at the hands of Christian nations, rulers, and missionaries. The Incarnational character of Jesus' Gospel has often not found its way into the life of the Church, either in relation to other religions or in relation to its own internal denominational history. Both internally and externally, borders and differences have been more characteristic of Christianity than have inclusiveness and acceptance.

More than one person has observed that the history of the Church does not speak well for the significance of the Gospel, since Jesus' followers do not actually follow his teachings. In response to the advice that we should not judge Jesus and his teachings by the failures of his followers one can only ask, "By what other standard are they to be judged ? Of what value is a teacher and his teachings if they are unable actually to be lived out by those who claim to be followers?" As Jesus himself said: "By their fruits you shall know them."

The good news is that throughout this rather sordid history there have always existed various exceptions, small pockets of Christians who have sought to be faithful to the Gospel of the Incarnation. Likewise, there have always been believers of other religions who have sought to be inclusive of those who nonetheless differ from themselves. Living faithfully on the borders dividing folks from one another is in fact possible, even though it is difficult. In the final chapters of this book we will look at two examples of Christians who have lived and practiced their faith in the borderlands, seeking peace, justice and inclusivity.

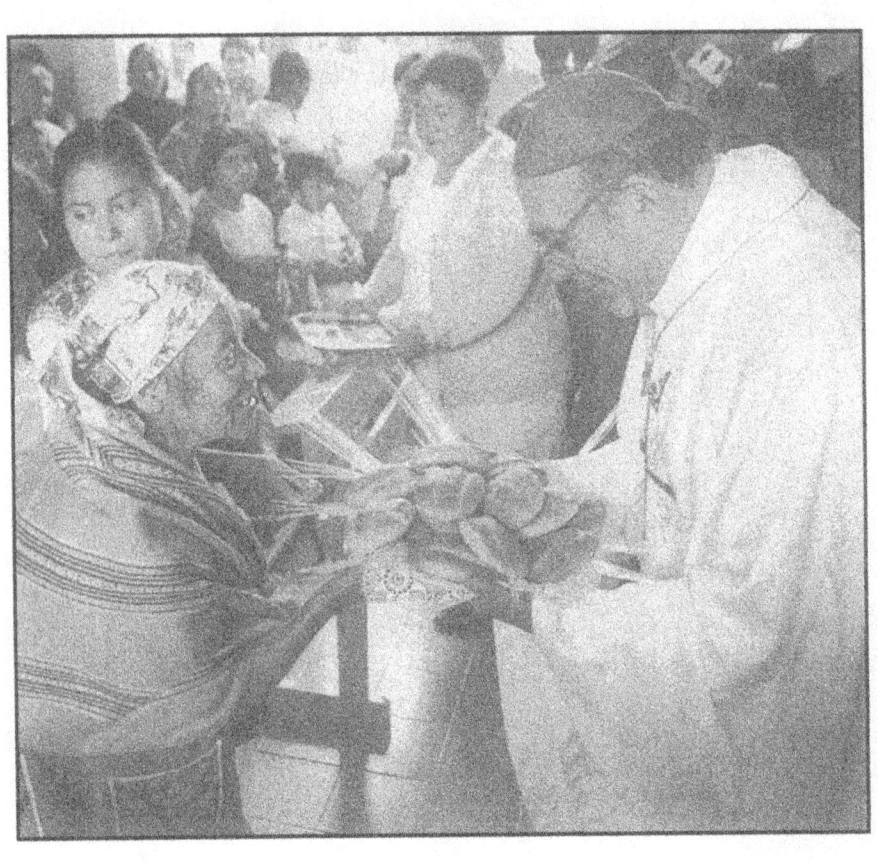

5

The Church in Chiapas, Mexico

The Ministry of Bishop Samuel Ruíz
In spite of the historic inability of the Christian Church to practice the kind of radical inclusiveness that Jesus taught, some Christians have understood the Incarnational Gospel and found ways to live a faithful and prophetic life in the borderlands. These Christians live all over the world and are engaged in the work of breaking down the barriers that divide us—barriers of class, sex, age, race, ethnicity, and religion. Some are the outsiders who cross geographical and class boundaries to challenge the wealthy and privileged. Others are insiders who give up their power and privilege to take sides with those who are excluded and oppressed.

The example I put forth in this chapter is that of Mexican Bishop Samuel Ruíz, who throughout his 40-year ministry as a bishop sought to embody and foster reconciliation among the varying social and political factions at work in the southern Mexican state of Chiapas. Bishop Ruíz retired in 1999 and the extent and quality of his service to the people of Chiapas has been powerfully focused in a book entitled *The People's Church* by Gary MacEoin (Crossroad Publishing, 1996).

Located in southeastern Mexico and bordering the country of Guatemala, Chiapas is the poorest state in Mexico. When Samuel Ruíz arrived there as a young bishop in January 1960, he found a place where barriers of class and race were as strong as anywhere on the continent. The 500-year old history of Spanish conquest and colonization had carved its rules of social hierarchy in this southern state as if into stone, and every power structure that existed—political, religious, social, and economic—functioned to reinforce that hierarchy.

As in the rest of Mexico there were strong social divisions by race in Chiapas, with a small number of white descendents of Spaniards or other Europeans on top of the hierarchy; mixed-blood people of both European and indigenous descent called *mestizos* in the middle; and indigenous people, often contemptuously called *indios*, at the bottom.

Unlike the majority of Mexico where *mestizos* now predominate, however, Chiapas is still 75% indigenous. Seven indigenous groups including the Tzeltal, the Tzotzil, the Tojolobal, the Chol, and the Mam live in the mountains, plains, and jungles of Chiapas. During the colonial period they were deprived of their lands, forced into hard labor, mistreated in many ways, and forced to convert to Catholicism. Early on, absurd debates took place in the Catholic Church about whether or not the Indians had souls, and while a few brave Church leaders such as Fray Bartolomé de las Casas spoke up for indigenous rights during colonial years, the overwhelming legacy of the colonial Catholic Church was the reinforcement of the idea of indigenous inferiority.

Mexico achieved independence from Spain in the early 1800s, but the colonial era left a lasting legacy of racism and economic exploitation. The new elite in Mexico City, mostly descended from the Spaniards, continued to treat the indigenous as second class citizens, and continued to view places like Chiapas primarily as a place from which to extract a wealth of natural resources. In the last 200 years, indigenous people in Chiapas have had only minimal access to health and education services. They have had to struggle constantly for land ownership, subsistence wages, and even minimal access to the justice system. They have been subject to the worst kinds of racism and abuse. It is a tribute to their perseverance and capacity to resist that the indigenous of Chiapas have survived and preserved their communities, language, and culture over the years.

The economic hierarchy in the state of Chiapas has been nearly as rigid as the racial hierarchy. While Chiapas is a state rich in oil, gas, hydroelectricity and timber, the wealth has always been controlled by a small minority of mostly *mestizo* landowners and businessmen, especially those with connections to the political party that was dominant for over 70 years, the Institutional Revolutionary Party (PRI).

Over the years, the federal government of Mexico has done more to extract wealth from Chiapas than to invest in human development for the people of the state. For example, while 60% of Mexico's hydroelectricity is produced in Chiapas, 35% of the people of Chiapas do not even have electricity in their homes. This percentage is even greater in the highlands where indigenous people live and, ironically, where the electricity is produced. In the early 1990s, 80% of homes in Chiapas had dirt floors, 80% had no potable water supply; 60% had no drainage system; 72% of students did not finish the first grade and 50% of the schools had only one teacher. These statistics, for the most part, reflect the living conditions of the indigenous of Chiapas.

Various laws over the years have facilitated some purchase of land by indigenous people, but many have been forced to work for subsistence wages or as sharecroppers on the large plantations and ranches of *mestizo* owners. This problem was somewhat ameliorated for several decades by an *ejido* system allowing community ownership of land consistent with indigenous culture and prohibiting sale to outside individual parties, but the *ejido* system was abolished in preparation for the North American Free Trade Agreement (NAFTA) between Mexico, the United States and Canada, which went into effect in January 1994. The elimination of the *ejido* took away the final safety net for indigenous people who, under great economic duress, have begun to sell their lands.

It should be noted that while Spanish colonial rule created the great gulfs between the "haves" and "have-nots" in Mexico, economic intervention and domination by the United States in the last century has also had an enormous effect in further aggravating the inequalities. U.S. business interests have had a heavy hand in the Mexican economy and have supported the highly corrupt political leadership. In addition, since the 1980s, the largest portion of Mexico's export earnings go to service its debts with foreign banks, many of them controlled by the United States. And now as "free" trade lowers barriers to foreign investment, it is increasingly the transnational corporations and a few billionaires who are benefiting from Mexico's riches. (At last count Mexico was fourth in the world in number of billionaires with 28.) Ironically, as the poor get poorer in Mexico, many leave their homelands to seek refuge and jobs in the United States.

The Church's Own Barriers

The Catholic Church was traditionally part of the ruling class in all of Latin America after the Spanish conquest. Allied with the political and economic colonial leadership, the Church's relationship with the indigenous poor was at best paternalistic and at worst defined by cultural genocide as it led the fight to extinguish native languages, practices, and religion. Religious, economic, and political power were so intertwined as to produce the kind of situation in which each wealthy Latin American was said to have wanted one son to be a governor, one son a landowner, and one son a priest. This kind of alliance was generally present in Mexico as well.

Indeed, until the early 1900s, the Church itself was a large landowner and almost completely identified with the landowning class. After the Mexican revolution which began in 1910, the Church fell out of favor with the State and lost its lands and much of its power but still retained important allies among the economic elite. It is accurate to say that in its nearly 500 years of history in Mexico, the Catholic Church tended to reinforce oppressive boundaries of race and class rather than speak out against them.

All of these boundaries were firmly in place in the southeastern state of Chiapas when Bishop Ruíz arrived on the scene, and when he began his ministry there, he did not question them. Ruíz, like very many of the priests and Bishops in Latin America, had been educated and trained in Rome to think of the Church as the guardian and dispenser of God's revealed truth. It was a time when Mass was still said in Latin, and the priest faced the altar rather than the congregation. The poor were not encouraged to read the Bible or think for themselves. Rather, they were to let the priest interpret any messages coming from the divine. They were not encouraged to think about God's will on earth, but rather to accept poverty as their fate and to eagerly await an afterlife where they would be relieved of their suffering.

All of this was about to change. The Catholic Church was about to experience a powerful awakening that would begin to turn around its practice of seeing the world through the eyes of the wealthy elite. Samuel Ruíz would take his place as a leader in the new Catholic Church, a Church that would choose a "preferential option for the poor."

In 1963, the Second Vatican Council (Vatican II) initiated changes in Catholic doctrine and practice that began to have wide-reaching effects. Many leaders in the Catholic Church began to recognize that the Church needed to become closer to its base, the majority of whom were poor. They set about to bridge the great divide that had been created between the masses of the faithful and the concept of the divine. After Vatican II, priests began to say mass in the native language of the congregation and to encourage lay people to form groups to read and think about the Bible on their own. They began to realize that for many people, this would first mean learning to read.

The Latin American Bishops conferences held in Medellín, Colombia, in 1968 and Puebla, Mexico, in 1979 helped extend the changes of Vatican II to Latin America and began to cultivate a fresh approach to the cultures and needs of indigenous people. In contrast to the previous arrogance of a Church somehow carrying the truth to ignorant natives, it was determined that the "seeds of the Gospel" were already present in the lives of all people because all are children of God and made in the Divine image.

The implications were deep. Changes in the Catholic Church were paralleling a tumultuous rise in revolutionary movements in which poor people all over the continent were demanding a change in the social, political and economic structures that oppressed them. When the Latin American Church went on to declare that the impoverishment and marginalization of the majority was not the will of God and could not be justified in light of the Gospel of Christ, the political, economic and racial elite of the continent began to feel threatened.

Of course 500 years of Church history was not to be changed overnight. Large sections of the Church feared any transfer of power to the poor and fought change every step of the way. Hundreds of priests and women religious, however, became vocal advocates for social justice and racial equality. A few bishops took those risks as well.

Samuel Ruíz Begins to Cross Borders
Bishop Ruíz was certainly influenced by Vatican II and the other changes in the Catholic Church, but even more importantly he allowed himself to be influenced by the reality of the people in his diocese. Shortly after his arrival in Chiapas in 1960, he made a decision to visit every town and village in the nearly 30,000 square miles that made up his diocese. Traveling often on horseback or by burro, he came face to face with the great poverty and disenfranchisement of the indigenous people.

At first the bishop did what anyone in his position would do on these kinds of trips; he stayed at the houses of the plantation owners. Soon however, he was challenged to go beyond that boundary, to accept hospitality in the shacks and hovels of the poor and to instruct his priests to do the same. The owners of the "big houses" felt rebuffed, threatened and even humiliated. The poor, on the other hand, began to trust Ruíz and to confide in him the reality of their lives. These crucial decisions made early in Ruíz's life as bishop eventually allowed him to rethink his entire understanding of the Church's role in Chiapas.

Under the leadership of Bishop Ruíz, the Diocese of Chiapas developed a ministry to the indigenous that became the most important ministry of the Church. Priests were asked to live in indigenous communities and to learn and value their languages and culture. They were instructed to build upon indigenous ideas and customs instead of counteracting them and to incarnate the gospel in the communities—in other words to learn to see Christ already present in their midst. Bishop Ruíz himself learned the Tzeltal and Tzotzil languages and developed a working knowledge of Tojolobal and Mam. He instructed his priests and catechists to learn to look at and tend to the physical needs of people in addition to their spiritual needs.

Literacy programs began and the Bible was translated into Tzeltal and Chol. Later in a combined effort with the Presbyterian Church, it was also translated to Tzotzil. As indigenous people were encouraged to form groups to study and comment on the Bible in light of their own experiences, it was not long before they began to identify with the Israelites enslaved in Egypt. Instead of viewing the Christian God as one who would have them suffer on earth, they began to think of a God whose desire it was to lead them out of slavery and into the promised land.

Based on these and other reflections, the Diocese of Chiapas developed a catechism resource for indigenous communities entitled *Estamos Buscando la Libertad*, or *We are Seeking Freedom*. As people began to organize to demand respect for their cultural identity and recognition for their autonomous governments, they were able to count on the Catholic Church as an ally. Confidence in church leaders grew to the point where indigenous communities no longer called their bishop "Señor Obispo" or "Monseñor" but rather began to call him a more familiar "Don Samuel" or even "Tatic," an affectionate indigenous word for father.

In 1974 the governor of Chiapas convened an Indigenous Congress and was surprised by the extent to which indigenous church activists took it over and organized it themselves. They made indigenous languages the official languages of the conference and turned it into a platform for people to speak about their needs. Among other things, people demanded the right to land and an end to the forced displacement of their communities by U.S. and Mexican timber companies. They demanded the rights to education, health, and transportation to sell their products.

Throughout the 1970s and 1980s, peasant, indigenous, and grassroots organization grew in Chiapas, and while much of this work was not directly related to the Church, the attempts by indigenous communities to assume control over their own destiny were looked upon favorably by the Church under Bishop Ruíz. This created tensions for Ruíz both with the local political powers in Chiapas and with the more conservative part of the Catholic Church. For them, the bishops had "changed sides" or turned against them. Ruíz's reversal of ministerial style and intent greatly upset the Catholic guardians of the Faith, both locally and in Rome, and more than once he was called on the carpet and threatened with removal for his crossing of conventional borders.

In the midst of all of its own turmoil, the state of Chiapas also had to face the unexpected arrival of large numbers of refugees from Guatemala. Between 1979 and 1983, some 40,000 refugees from poor indigenous communities in Guatemala fled into Chiapas and surrounding areas to escape the genocide and scorched earth policies of Guatemalan military dictators. They arrived traumatized and without food, clothing, shelter, or money. On at least one occasion the refugees were attacked by the Guatemalan army, even on Mexican soil. Slowly and at the urging of the Diocese of Chiapas, whose priests had begun to attend to the refugees almost immediately, the Mexican government and the United Nations moved in to protect the refugees.

The refugees stayed in Mexico for almost 15 years, creating major social issues for states like Chiapas that carried most of the burden. The presence of the Guatemalans drained resources for local people and depressed wages in the area. It would have been easy for the people of Chiapas to have scorned the refugees or resented the assistance they received. But Bishop Ruíz's Church once again set the standard for tearing down the walls of exclusion. Church workers emphasized the need to attend to the refugees, protect their human and economic rights, and see them as brothers and sisters.

Human Rights Ministry

Crossing entrenched boundaries and borders is never easy. Predictably, the elite of Chiapas felt threatened, and despite Church efforts at education and reconciliation, the local political bosses began to use their official and extra-official authority to lash out at those who threatened their power. In response, the Diocese created the Fray Bartolomé de las Casas Human Rights Center, named after a 16th century bishop who had fought hard with the Vatican to try to end the brutal exploitation of the indigenous people in colonial times.

The Human Rights Center opened in 1989 and presented documentation of 4,732 cases of repressive action by public authority between 1974 and 1987. These included acts of murder, torture, theft, and repression of protest. As repression increased, Bishop Ruíz was gradually forced to move his defense of indigenous people to national and international arenas through the work of the Fray Bartolomé de las Casas Human Rights Center. To this day the Human Rights

Center continues to function, denouncing acts of violence and repression. It is the most respected human rights organization in Chiapas, and its findings have been corroborated by Amnesty International and other groups.

When the Pope came to visit Mexico in 1993, Don Samuel presented him with a long letter in which he documented the conditions under which the indigenous people were forced to live, as well as the reasons for why these conditions existed. His letter to the Pope received a great deal of attention in the media, both within and beyond Mexico, and created alarm among those who had been working to improve the image of Mexico for the passage of NAFTA.

As pressure increased, it is quite likely that Bishop Ruíz would have been removed from office, either by the Church or by the political leaders of Chiapas, had it not been for a highly unexpected turn of events: the uprising of the Zapatista Army of National Liberation (EZLN) on January 1, 1994.

Led by the mysterious and charismatic Subcomandante Marcos, this rebel army came out of the Chiapan jungle on New Years Day and occupied over a half dozen towns in the highlands. Some of the rebels carried weapons of war, but many of them carried only sticks or hunting rifles. Some wore boots; others had tattered shoes or were barefoot. They wore cheap army uniforms and covered their faces with bandanas or ski masks. Quietly and quickly they took over four cities. In the town of San Cristóbal, where Ruíz had his offices, they occupied buildings, cut phone lines, and released prisoners.

A Spanish-speaking man wearing a ski mask emerged as a spokesperson and identified himself as Subcomandante Marcos. He read the *Declaration of the Lacandón Rainforest*, in which the Zapatistas declared war on the Mexican State and put forth their 12 demands: freedom, democracy, justice, peace, land, education, health, housing, food, development, cultural rights and women's rights. By stating these demands, the Zapatistas were letting the world know that the most basic human rights were still not accessible to a majority of people in Chiapas, and they were demanding a say in their own future.

The Zapatistas were effective in their press work and in a matter of minutes, the news of the rebellion had spread throughout the world on faxes sent out from the humble offices of a local San Cristóbal newspaper. People in Latin America, the United States and Europe were soon reading about the centuries of oppression suffered by the indigenous peoples of Chiapas, and about the Zapatistas' 12 demands. Thus, when the Mexican Army responded violently to put down the rebellion, international pressure mounted to demand respect for human rights and negotiations with the Zapatista rebels.

The Zapatista uprising was a response to 500 years of oppression, but it was timed to coincide with the date that the North American Free Trade Agreement (NAFTA) was to take effect: January 1, 1994. In his first communique Subcomandante Marcos charged that NAFTA signed a "death certificate for the indigenous people of Mexico." Indeed, as a prerequisite for admission into NAFTA, Mexico had done away with the Article 27 of its constitution which had guaranteed indigenous people the right to hold and farm in common large areas of land called *ejidos*. By privatizing all land, the NAFTA agreement made it both possible and necessary for individual farmers to sell their land to larger land owners and developers. As if to assure the displacement of traditional farmers, this "free" trade agreement also allowed the massive influx of corn and other grains from the United States, which flooded the market and forced down the prices of the products that the indigenous farmers traditionally sold. "Free" trade also eliminated the little government support that existed for coffee farmers, leaving them at the mercy of private middlemen to sell their products. In effect the indigenous poor were being asked to abandon their farmlands and cultural heritage and to take jobs in the urban, foreign-owned factories that would be arriving courtesy of NAFTA.

While the initial reaction of the Mexican Government to the Zapatistas was to retaliate, international attention to civilian deaths and human rights violations forced them to back off and turn to negotiations. Thus a standoff developed between the EZLN and the Mexican national government, and Bishop Ruíz was chosen to be the mediator and chief negotiator of a peace. Suddenly the one blamed for instigating unrest was now to be the one to calm it.

So once again Bishop Ruíz found himself living on the border between two antagonistic forces, trying to find a way to help them overcome their differences. Although he clearly was in agreement with the Zapatistas about the justice of their cause on behalf of the indigenous people, he was equally sure that the solution to this confrontation should not involve violence and death. Fortunately, the Zapatistas were using their weapons more as a way to call attention to their plight than for the purpose of taking over the government. They consistently pressed for the democratic restructuring of the Mexican socioeconomic system to meet their demands.

Negotiations and the Legacy of Bishop Ruíz

The next years saw massive organization by the Zapatistas and their civilian base. More than 1,100 villages in 34 municipalities organized themselves as "communities in resistance" or "autonomous communities." They are not separatist and do consider themselves part of Mexico, but Zapatista autonomous communities work independently of federal and state government and have their own economic, judicial and political systems. They elect their authorities by consensus, have a system for collective work and community service, and look to develop according to community needs rather than by the decrees of the federal government and corporate interests.

At first, negotiations seemed to support these efforts and under the leadership of Bishop Ruíz, an initial peace accord was signed in February 1996 between the Zapatistas and the federal government of Mexico. The accord was specifically on the issue Indigenous Rights and Culture and it recognized indigenous autonomy and control over the natural resources in their areas. Unfortunately, the Mexican government refused to take the next step of signing these accords into law and soon negotiations broke down.

Instead, indigenous areas of Chiapas have been militarized by the Mexican Army. Military presence and related paramilitary activity have costs the lives of hundreds of indigenous poor. Even heightened international presence has not been able to end this violence. At one point it was hoped that the standoff would be resolved by the newly elected Mexican President, Vicente Fox. Although Fox did invite the Zapatistas to the Capitol where they were allowed to address the National Congress, little else has come of these events.

Through these many years, the Catholic Church of Chiapas and some of its Protestant allies continued to educate and mobilize for a peace with justice. In 1997, *Las Abejas*, an indigenous Catholic pacifist group that supports Zapatista ideals, paid an especially high price for their commitment to active nonviolence. Paramilitary groups with government ties swept into their community and massacred 45 men, women, and children in the highlands village of Acteal.

If this story were made for a novel or a movie, the forces of justice and righteousness would have triumphed despite the odds against them. Bishop Ruíz would have been able to negotiate an end to the violence and the Mexican government would have changed the policies that crush the poor and indigenous of Chiapas. Unfortunately, this has not been the case. After presiding over the funeral in Acteal, Bishop Ruíz resigned from the National Intermediation Commission in protest in 1998. The commission disbanded, and after years of on-again, off-again meetings, there has been no further progress in talks.

In Chiapas today, *mestizo* society, local aristocracies, land owners, and political functionaries continue to play the role of highly privileged insiders, along with the powerful transnational corporations. The indigenous are still the outsiders, struggling to keep from losing the little they have had. Samuel Ruíz was required to submit his resignation as bishop in 1999 when he turned 75, the forces of free trade continue to dictate the policies of Mexico, and the struggle continues in Chiapas.

This is a sober reminder that crossing unjust human barriers will not necessarily make you a winner in the conventional sense. Rendering the Word into flesh is a painful and risky undertaking, as the Incarnation of Jesus Christ clearly shows. It remains, however, the task of those who would be faithful. And while Samuel Ruíz—like Moses and like Christ—may never see the promised land, hope lies in the assurance that the promised land still lies ahead.

The Borderland Nature of Bishop Ruíz's Ministry

Bishop Ruíz practiced his Borderland Theology in many ways. First and foremost he crossed the boundaries of his privilege and power to work on the same level as the people whom he and his coworkers served. Embodying the Incarnational love of God, he did not wait for the people to come to him. Rather, he journeyed to where they were to meet them on their own terms.

Secondly, Bishop Ruíz was a borderland theologian in his attempts to extend the Church's ministry beyond the spiritual to include the physical. In his Incarnation, Jesus Christ moved from the divine to the human. He became vulnerable to the needs of the flesh. He was hungry and thirsty. He needed rest and warm clothing. As Bishop Ruíz and his priests slept on the hard, bug-infested, dirt floors of the homes of the indigenous poor, they understood anew the importance of Christ's work in feeding the hungry and healing the sick. When the people of Chiapan parishes asked quite straightforwardly if the Gospel applied to matters of the body as well as to those of the soul, Bishop Ruíz was listening with a new ear, and his deeds answered with a resounding "Yes."

Thirdly, while not ignoring the humanity or concerns of the oppressors, Bishop Ruíz refused to accept as permanent the religious and political structures of oppression and exploitation. He saw God's love and grace as all-inclusive and unconditional, and for him this meant that every barrier separating peoples from one another was wrong in God's eyes. Just as Jesus included women and children and Samaritans, Bishop Ruíz sought to include the poor, the indigenous, and the oppressed, by helping them to find a permanent place in the decisions that influenced their own lives.

Bishop Ruíz did his best to break down the barriers between insiders and outsiders in God's parish. In his view, the Church—like ancient Israel and the early Jewish Christians—has been far too quick to forget they had at first been wanderers, immigrants, and outsiders. Bishop Ruíz sought to weave a web of inclusiveness and to carry out a mission that bridges borders. In this way he stands as a paradigmatic example of an agent of reconciliation in the midst of the divisive if not demonic powers that surround him and his people.

Collaboration and conversation with Protestant churches is another example of Bishop Ruiz's willingness to cross borders. Ecumenism is not strong in Latin America and Chiapas is no exception, yet Bishop Ruiz's Catholic Church collaborated with the Presbyterian Church and others in efforts to translate the Bible into indigenous languages and to address the very immediate needs of the poor.

Finally, a borderland theologian does not assume that he or she has the entire truth, but rather looks beyond him or herself to hear other voices and perspectives. Bishop Ruíz did this by listening to indigenous communities and to the just demands of the Zapatista movement. He placed himself as a mediator in the discussions between the Zapatistas and the government, not as someone who would go through the motions and pretend to hear what they had to say in order to go back to the status quo, but as one who would actually lift up their legitimate demands and work to negotiate a real change. He was leader in an unfinished process of deep reconciliation.

Borderland Theology, like the Liberation Theology that emerged in Latin America in the years following Vatican II, stresses the freeing power of God's love of humanity and justice in overcoming the bondage of oppressed and exploited people. These emphases were the seeds which have begun to bloom in the efforts of the people of Chiapas to participate in the shaping of their own destiny. At the very least they have provided the soil from which the Zapatista uprising has taken root.

While there is no direct connection between the Liberation Theology practiced by Samuel Ruiz's Catholic Church in Chiapas and the birth of the Zapatista movement, one could argue that there is an *indirect* causal connection. It seems probable that the new direction of the Diocese under Bishop Ruíz helped to quicken the indigenous people's political and social awareness in a manner congruent with the concerns of the Zapatistas.

In short, Ruíz's ministry gave rise to the strong sense of self-worth and dignity among the indigenous people upon which the Zapatistas built as they formulated and implemented their own political endeavors. For decades Ruíz and his many pastoral workers strove to take the cultures, languages, and ideas of the people in Chiapas seriously and to instill a participatory approach toward spirituality and Church life. In so doing Ruíz almost completely reversed the traditional hierarchical procedures of the Catholic Church.

John Womack Jr., the author of *Rebellion in Chiapas*, summarizes Bishop Ruiz's view of the changes he made in the following way: "In his opinion the main change in the diocese is that the Indian poor have had a *toma de consciencia*. This would be a mighty change. *Tomar consciencia* is to take cognizance, to question received faith, wisdom, and conventions, to become conscious in a new frame of mind that people, things, qualities, may not be as they had seemed or been supposed to be, to try to discover, recognize, know them as they truly are, and in this knowledge accept explicitly the obligations of conscience to do good. It is a powerful mental and moral experience, which especially strengthens the capacity to organize with others to make the wrong right." (p.23)

The Zapatista Example

Bishop Ruíz is no longer the leader of the Catholic Church in Chiapas, but the changes that happened under his term as Bishop continue to have their effect. It is unlikely that indigenous communities who have dreamed of autonomy and control over their own lives will ever return quietly to being submissive servants of the elite. And leaders of the Catholic Church continue to accompany indigenous communities as they search for new ways to express their struggle for equality and justice.

In addition, the Zapatista example remains, seeking to call Mexico and all modern nations back to certain values that lie at the heart of viable and meaningful human life. With a fresh, yet enduring voice, Marcos's communiques combine serious concerns with quixotic irony and self-effacing humor. Zapatistas continue to strive to be the voice of a value system of an "enchanted" or ideal world that demands dignity, inclusion, and justice for all people. In the imagery offered by Walter Benjamin in Adolfo Gilly's book, *Rural Revolt in Mexico*, the Zapatista rebellion seeks to "throw the emergency brake" on the human train that is hurling Mexico, as well as the rest of the world, headlong into a dehumanizing, exclusive, and oppressive form of modernity.

Adolfo Gilly argues that the Zapatistas have risen up in the midst of the indigenous jungle to call into question not modernity itself, but the exclusive and unilateral manner in which it is being perpetrated on the Third World. The Zapatistas are not opposed to all change or modernity. Their deliberate inclusion of women into the leadership of the autonomous communities is a sign of this willingness to reflect critically on their own traditions. But Zapatistas want to have a say in how the changes in their lives will occur, and according to what values. They call for all Mexican citizens, as well as citizens of the world at large, to participate in holding the Mexican government to its responsibilities as expressed in the original Mexican Constitution.

The voice from the "enchanted world," from the heart of humanity itself and encapsulated in the radical Christian message, does not call the world back to some romantic, pre-modern place. It calls, rather, to insist that the modernization of the whole world be grounded in the dignity and full participation of all people. As in the post-apocalyptic world of the movie *Beyond Thunderdome* where all relationships are reduced to violent struggles in the Thunderdome arena between those with power and those without, the indigenous peoples of the Latin American world are singing with Tina Turner: "We don't need another hero, we don't need to find the way home; all we want is a way beyond Thunderdome."

6

The Church in a Mission of Reconciliation

Bridging Borders

This final chapter offers a look at another unique effort at practicing Borderland Theology, this time along the border of two countries: Mexico and the United States. Here we focus on the work of an organization called BorderLinks as an inspiring example of how people of faith have sought to bridge the gaps of exclusion and domination. BorderLinks is a not-for-profit organization that has provided experiential educational opportunities along the United States-Mexico border since 1988. Its mission is to raise awareness among people of the United States about the realities of life and work on the border, realities that encompass every aspect of human existence from the socio-political to the economic and religious.

BorderLinks grew out of the "Sanctuary Movement" begun by U.S. churches and synagogues in the 1980s. The Sanctuary Movement brought Central American political refugees across the border and helped them to find the safe haven and support they needed in the United States at a time when the U.S. government was denying them political asylum. As the flow of refugees subsided, however, a number of people remained concerned about the many difficulties on the U.S.-Mexico border, and they took steps to make sure these issues were kept alive in discussion and action.

In 1988 the Tucson Refugee Support Group linked with two groups on the east coast to provide ongoing education about the U.S.-Mexico border. This supporting group of advisors hired a young man named Rick Chase, who had indicated a strong interest in border education on a part-time basis. His job was to try to bring people from the Atlantic Coast region of the United States to the U.S.-Mexico border as participants in short-term travel seminars. Rick, the son of a Presbyterian minister and a graduate of Colorado College, had been to Nicaragua with a Witness for Peace delegation a few years before and was committed to helping North Americans understand what it is about their own lives, both personal and corporate, that contributes to the severe difficulties faced by people living in Latin America.

While in Nicaragua, Rick was so moved by the plight of the people there that he told his indigenous peasant host that God was calling him to go home, learn Spanish, and return to help the Nicaraguans. His host looked him in the eye and said, "My friend, you have misunderstood the call of God. What you should do is go home and help your own people see how they are helping to cause the problems you see here." Rick did as the man directed, and answered instead a call to border education.

The first travel seminar took place in January 1988. By June 1989 Rick had obtained funding for himself as a Mission Volunteer for the National Office of the Presbyterian Church and moved his base of operations from Philadelphia to Tucson. He was replaced in the east coast office by Kitty Ufford. Eventually Kitty, too, moved to Tucson where she and Rick were later married. With the help of the Tucson support group they began to organize and lead an increasing number of trips across and along the border and BorderLinks was on its way.

The United States-Mexico Border

Radical changes occurred in Mexico during the 1980s and 1990s, largely as a result of the country's efforts to become a participant in the new global economy. Large export- oriented agribusiness swallowed up small farms in Central Mexico, displacing hundreds of thousands of peasant farmers. Meanwhile, the NAFTA free trade agreement allowed manufacturers from the United States to build more assembly-line factories for textile, clothing, and electronic exports all along the Mexican side of the U.S.-Mexico border.

Some of the jobs that were lost to farmers were replaced by jobs in these factories—called *maquiladoras* in Spanish—and as the Mexican economy flagged in other areas, literally millions of Mexicans began moving to the border to find work.

Not only does this new economic pattern mean that people are no longer able to grow their own food and that they must uproot themselves from their native area, but it also means that they are pretty much forced to compete for work in these border factories for wages that amount to about $1.00 per hour. Because the cost of living along the border is not much lower on the Mexican side than it is on the U.S. side, two or more people in every family must work simply to pay for the basic necessities of life.

These difficulties are greatly exacerbated by several additional factors. The simple fact is that none of the border towns along the Mexican side can possibly keep up with the influx of people seeking work. Thus thousands of migrants arrive in towns like Nogales, Sonora with no place to live except in squatter communities, or *colonias*, few of which even have running water, electricity, and sewage facilities. Moreover, the Mexican Government fails to provide such services without political coercion, partly because the political process is quite corrupt, but also because funds are scarce. Mexico does have its billionaires, but the vast majority of its people are extremely poor. Since under the new organization of the economy, money is increasingly going into already wealthy private hands instead of to the government, there is little money for public works projects.

The conditions of the NAFTA agreement do not require the owners of the *maquiladoras* to bear any responsibility for their worker's welfare. They take advantage of the unlimited amount of very cheap labor and pay only minimal or no taxes to the local governments whose facilities are being overcrowded by the onslaught of people looking for work. Although some companies do attempt to provide such amenities as cafeterias and daycare centers, most do not. Moreover, the workers must operate on a bonus system and comply with strict rules if they wish to keep their jobs. It is extremely difficult for workers to form unions or try to raise wages in any way. Not only are there plenty of unemployed people ready to take the low-paying jobs, factories can also simply close up shop and move to another country with even cheaper labor should workers become too "troublesome." Since the year 2000 many *maquiladoras* in Mexico have, in fact, moved to Asian countries where they can pay workers even less.

What is so tragically ironic about all this is that it is done in the name of "free enterprise." The parts of the clothing or electronic devices that these workers assemble go back and forth across the border, as do the large profits accrued by the owners, but the workers themselves are not able to cross the border freely to get better jobs. They are merely a cheap and captive work force.

Not only do those living along the Mexican side of the border have to deal with severe poverty and abysmal working conditions, but in large measure it is free market policies that create this situation. Because most of us in the United States want cheaper products and produce, and because the quest for profits strongly outweighs social and moral considerations in the current global economy, U.S. citizens and our government are major players in causing the pain and suffering of countries like Mexico. This is the reality we face.

BorderLinks

It was against this backdrop that BorderLinks got under way. Under the guidance of Rick Chase, who as the result of his marriage to Kitty Ufford had become Rick Ufford-Chase, the tiny organization was fashioned into an educational enterprise that focuses on experiential education around the socio-political issues of the border. Throughout the 1990s an ever-increasing number of groups, mostly from churches, seminaries, and colleges, participated in BorderLinks trips. During this time Rick received advice and support from such well-known theologians and activists as Robert and Sidney McAfee Brown, Richard Schaull, Nancy Johns, and Mary Ann Lundy.

BorderLinks grew quickly during the last half of the 1990s. The staff went from four to 22, eight of whom are Mexican nationals working on the Mexican side of the border. (Three of these are Catholic Sisters.) The annual budget increased from $200,000 to over $800,000 and the small group of advisors was transformed into a 22 person steering committee made up of local educators, bankers, lawyers, activists, and ministers.

The programs of BorderLinks have become as diverse as its staff, advisors, and supporters. At the facility in Nogales, Mexico, named *Casa de La Misericordia* or "House of Mercy," the local staff provides lunch for more than 300 children a day, distributes clothing to their parents, and administers grants that have been procured to help establish micro-credit banking among some of the women, as well workshops for environmental education in various Mexican communities, a food cooperative, and various gardening and composting projects. In addition, a regular Semester on the Border program for college students partners with over a dozen schools around the country to provide courses in Mexican History, Peace and Justice, Liberation Theology, Culture of the Borderlands, and Spanish.

Travel Seminars

All of the above programs are significant, but the heart of the work of BorderLinks are the travel seminars where U.S.-Americans are brought face to face with the hard realities of border life and the factors that contribute to their existence. Although there really is no "typical" trip run by BorderLinks—some last for only a few days while others continue for two or three weeks—there are certain key elements that are included in each BorderLinks experience.

Every group begins with a period of orientation to the border, to BorderLinks, and to the members of the group itself. Such orientations generally include conversations with someone from the Border Patrol, a local history professor who explains the history of the border, a local lawyer who relates the difficulties surrounding immigration policies, with John Fife who tells the story of the Sanctuary Movement, and a local refugee from Central America or Mexico.

The majority of these conversations take place in Tucson, Arizona where BorderLinks is based. After crossing over the border into Mexico, the groups generally visit a *maquiladora*, various social service centers that seek to help children, and several *colonias*, where travel seminar participants meet, talk, and have meals with the people living in these squatter communities. Usually arrangements have been made for the visitors from the United States to spend at least one night if not several with one of these Mexican families in their shanty town home made from cinder blocks, cardboard, and tin set up on a dirt floor. The meals consist primarily of tortillas and beans.

An additional feature of the trips is the "market basket survey" where participants confront the cost of living on the Mexican side of the border by going to the local market and finding out what the various items on a typical shopping list actually cost. Also, at various times each day a period is set aside for group reflection on the significance of a key scriptural passage, usually from the Gospels, for the realities being encountered along the way. One of Jesus' parables about workers in the fields or the story of Jesus visiting a community on the other side of the Sea of Galilee are frequently used for these sessions. Often the focus is on the meaning of his request, "Let's go over to the other side" as it pertains to crossing the border.

Those trips that last several days often involve travel a bit deeper into Mexico or further along the border to Agua Prieta or Ciudad Juarez just south of El Paso, Texas. Every few days such groups stop over at a hotel in order to shower and rest up from the rather grueling and discouraging aspects of this type of experience. The final two or three days are usually devoted to a group reflection on the total experience of the journey and to a discussion of the question "So what?" That is to say, now that we have seen the realities of the border and know something of its causes, what can and will we do about it when we return home?

It is not the intention of BorderLinks to browbeat its often middle-class, white participants or to produce a heavy burden of guilt and pathos about the border reality. It is, rather, to aid in finding ways to better understand this situation and to set about doing something that might just make a positive difference. In fact, seminar participants almost invariably find the travel seminars to be transforming experiences, and in their final reflections they often commit to a number of things including: living more simply, organizing a group of concerned citizens in their church or neighborhood, or lobbying their congressional representatives. One thing is clear: Those who dare to cross borders with their eyes wide open do not go back the same people.

Through such journeys, then, BorderLinks helps build bridges across one specific division in the world today, the one between the United States and Mexico. It is a particularly dramatic crossing because the border that separates these two countries is the only place where you can move from the First World into the Third World in one simple step. The huge metal wall that divides Nogales, Arizona, from Nogales, Sonora, keeps Mexican people from entering the United States and stands as a symbolic and literal barrier. It is a barrier to reconciliation. Thus the border becomes a metaphor, not only for all the economic borders in the world, but also for every other sort of barrier that we construct between insiders and outsiders.

An Educational Vision
Over the last 12 years thousands of people from dozens of schools and churches all over the United States have participated in BorderLinks travel seminars, and hundreds of others have contributed financially to help make such trips possible. In a recent capital campaign to raise money for the purchase of a highly useful campus in Nogales, Sonora, there were over a thousand contributors with an average gift of $875. The goal of the campaign was $250,000 and in seven months it had been exceeded by nearly fifty percent. Above all else it was the integrity of the BorderLinks organization that was responsible for such enthusiastic giving.

The educational philosophy that drives BorderLinks comes primarily from three sources. Rick's initial inspiration came from liberation theologian, Gustavo Gutiérrez, who urged those who wish to learn about life and serve those in need to stay close to the lives and struggles of the poor. The specifics of the educational process employed in the actual reflection opportunities in BorderLinks seminars are borrowed in large part from the ideas of Paulo Freire's well-known work *Pedagogy of the Oppressed.*

The focus of Freire's book is the notion of "consciousness raising" which, as the root of the key term indicates, also entails the raising of one's conscience. This experience is one in which a person's basic way of perceiving and understanding the world is transformed in both depth and breadth. Freire encouraged learners to "experience, reflect, act, and evaluate" each and every process and situation in which they find themselves, thus creating an ongoing learning dynamic involving every aspect of a person's life.

The third source for the BorderLinks educational vision derives from the life and work of Myles Horton, who founded and, from the 1930s to the 1950s, directed the Highlander Center in the mountains of Tennessee. Horton's goal was to find ways to bring education for life to workers, farmers, and minority peoples, especially in the rural South. His life story and philosophy are powerfully captured in his book *The Long Haul.* The key to this type of education is to work together with others as fellow learners rather than to try to impose some presupposed understanding of a situation on them.

Such participatory and democratic policies have found their way into the BorderLinks experiential educational practice in various ways. Every effort is made to provide those participating in the travel seminars with a broad exposure to as many different perspectives on border life as possible—from that of the Border Patrol and *maquiladora* management to political activists and indigenous workers. Moreover, in the participants' reflections and discussions, the insights of each person are important. The idea is to "experience, reflect, act, and evaluate" together and to enrich the process by doing so.

The educational philosophy and process, however, is not only for the people from the United States who are the travel seminar participants. The Mexican people who receive the trip participants in their homes and workplaces are also a vital part of the ongoing dialogue. BorderLinks' contacts in Mexico are indigenous educators and learners in their own right, and their experiences and views constitute a crucial dimension of what BorderLinks is about. Over the years Rick and other staff members have sought and cultivated close relationships with dozens of individuals and groups in Mexico, who in turn have become the interactive partners of the U.S. residents who come learn about the realities of the border.

BorderLinks' educational bridges are comprised of a two-way exchange or dynamic that allows mutual interaction and learning to take place. Those who dwell in the squatter communities, as well as those working in Christian "base communities" on the Mexican side of the border are active in seeking to understand and improve their own situation and naturally there is much to learn from them. Among other projects, they have developed micro-credit banking groups and a cooperative market. From Ciudad Juarez to Agua Prieta and Nogales, BorderLinks has a great number of partners in education that provide both a bilateral learning experience and a binational perspective.

Between 1998 and 2002, BorderLinks was blessed by the addition of several Mexican nationals to the staff including a husband and wife team who coordinate the cooperative market and soon-to-be child center. Three others are Sisters of the Missionaries of the Eucharist based in Guadalajara, Mexico, while another is a woman who has worked for years as a Catholic social worker and is a long-time friend of BorderLinks. In addition, BorderLinks is incorporated as a not-for-profit organization in Mexico and has recently purchased a campus facility in Nogales, Sonora.

From this Mexican base of operations it not only runs its regular programs, but is engaged in developing new ways to both educate and assist people on the Mexican side of the border with programs that enable them to develop their own insights and resources for dealing with the specific problems they encounter. Because of this base in Mexico, it is increasingly possible to bring people from both sides of the border together in conferences and workshops to share their reflections, ideas, and proposals.

In some ways the most remarkable aspect of the BorderLinks enterprise is the extremely high caliber of those who have chosen to work in it. The responsibilities of organizing the office, recruiting and planning for visiting groups, actually leading individual trips along the border, and fundraising lie in the hands of about a dozen highly talented and dedicated persons. In the past the great majority of staff members have been recent college graduates, but recently several people making mid-life career changes have come on board.

Although there is a certain amount of turnover at the actual program level among the staff, there is now a strong tendency to develop a longer commitment among core staff and allow Rick Ufford-Chase, now the International Director, to devote his time to administration, planning, and public relations. There are now two regional Directors, one for the Mexican side of the border and one for the U.S. side. Gender barriers, age barriers, and race barriers are all bridged on the BorderLinks staff. There are two members over 60 years of age, with most others being between 25 and 45. In the year 2002, there are 10 males on staff and 18 females, including 14 Mexicans, and 14 U.S.-Americans. Such diverse distribution is quite intentional.

Throughout the years a highly active and broad group of people has always cooperated with BorderLinks by providing both advice and material support. In recent years this commitment and energy have taken the form of a Board of Directors who meet bimonthly to discuss and decide policy matters. The board reaches decisions through a process of discussion and consensus. Here, too, a genuine effort is made to bridge national, gender, age, and racial barriers. The same can be said for the six professors who make up the faculty of the semester program; three of these are Hispanic and three are Anglo. In both groups a range of religious beliefs, including Catholic, Quaker, Presbyterian, Jewish, Mormon, Mennonite, and agnostic, is also represented.

The Tenth Anniversary Conference

One of the real highpoints of the BorderLinks story was the conference held in 1998 to celebrate its first ten years of ministry. This adventure began with the BorderLinks sponsorship of four 5-day excursions to different Central American countries, along with one to Chiapas, Mexico, and another to the U.S.-Mexico border itself. In each case these delegations were joined by people from local cooperating organizations.

The purpose of these trips was to allow delegates from different corners of the United States to experience first-hand what was going on in Central America and Mexico so that they could all then come together at the conference on the border to share their respective reports, insights, and proposals. The focus was on the effect of the global economy on the people in these areas and what might be done about it.

The conference began with Catholic Bishop Thomas Gumbleton of Detroit delivering the keynote address at a local church in Tucson. The next morning all 300 participants from the United States were bused to Nogales, Sonora, where they joined with many Mexican nationals and delegates from other Latin American countries. The delegates shared their experiences and ideas in the morning and after lunch various taskforces met to plan future actions. The event concluded with a festive dinner-dance.

This event was a gigantic success, both in its own right and in the overall story of BorderLinks. It provided a unique opportunity for people of the United States and Latin America to come together at the border and exchange knowledge, values, and ideas. BorderLinks is looking forward to sponsoring more such events in the near future, organized around specific themes such as theology and economics, immigration, and grassroots movement building. All such conferences will be ecumenical, multiracial and multinational. Sadly, because of the exclusive nature of our border, it is nearly impossible to hold such conferences on the U.S. side. The lack of economic resources and visas would keep many Latin American participants out.

Ongoing Developments
Other examples of BorderLinks' border-crossing endeavors bear mentioning. One is that of two folk musicians—one white and one Latino—who go into rural or poor urban squatters' communities on the Mexican side of the border and teach children to gather stories from the local elders in order to create and perform songs from them. These two men are extremely gifted and genuine in their love for both elders and children. Their ministry promises to grow into an important part of what BorderLinks is about all along the border—the crossing of both age and cultural boundaries with music.

Another creative example of the BorderLinks program includes the recent purchase of a former school bus to be used by both BorderLinks and other groups as transportation to and from various conferences, peace demonstrations, and other events that seek to bridge the gulfs between and among people everywhere. The bus has crossed many state and national borders, uniting people from many different places, backgrounds and religions. On the sides of the bus are painted the words: "Education on the Move."

By far the most dramatic aspect of the BorderLinks ongoing program is the already alluded to acquisition of the site that is now called *Casa de la Misericordia* (House of Mercy). Over a period of years, a Mexican couple built and maintained this campus site in the midst of several lower economic *colonias* as a place to feed lunch to the many children of the area who have no place to get a hot meal in the day time. They also distributed clothes to the people of the nearby neighborhoods.

After the husband died, his widow informed Rick that she wanted to sell the Casa to some group, like BorderLinks, that would see to it that the lunch program for the children would continue and that other related programs would be developed. Rick and the rest of the BorderLinks staff and board were delighted. Here was an opportunity not only to expand the ministry of BorderLinks across the border into Mexico, but to become more closely involved with the people of Nogales, Sonora, themselves; both physical and cultural walls could be overcome.

It was not long before plans were under way to raise the necessary funds to purchase the Casa, and within a few months this purchase became a reality. Uppermost in the minds of those working with BorderLinks in this project is the need to move slowly and carefully so as not to be yet one more group of gringo do-gooders who come across the border to show the "poor Mexicans" how things should be done. BorderLinks is not primarily a direct service organization. It is an educational and activist organization that seeks to learn from others as much as it seeks to help them.

Since the Casa has traditionally served as a form of direct service, however, BorderLinks is committed to continuing this ministry, adding to it with self-help workshops and other educational tools. The hope is that by being grounded in the reality of people's daily needs through direct service, the educational and activist parts of BorderLink's work can be strengthened.

The most recent, and in the long run perhaps the most significant, major development in the BorderLinks overall mission has been the hosting of international *encuentros* or gatherings. In the spring of 2002 BorderLinks conducted two major binational conferences at the *Casa Misericordia* which were attended by more than eighty participants, the majority of whom were from Mexico. These were followed by other gatherings throughout 2002 and 2003.

The first of these *encuentros* focused on understanding the global economy and was facilitated by some leaders from a "popular economics" organization. The conference lasted from a Friday evening through supper on Saturday and involved several different workshops and lectures. Not only did a majority of participants learn a great deal, but the bilingual, binational character of this gathering was as invigorating as it was innovative. The second *encuentro* centered on the Biblical notion of Jubilee, wherein the people of God were instructed to return all land to its original owner, cancel all debts, and free captive servants. The year of Jubilee was meant to take place once every 50 years in Old Testament times and was instituted in order to avoid gross inequalities among various groups of people. The conference was led by Ross and Gloria Kinsler, retired seminary professors from Costa Rica.

This aspect of the BorderLinks adventure has long been Rick's special dream since it epitomizes an extremely important dimension of the challenge to cross borders and bridge barriers in the name of God's Incarnational activity. To actually bring together a large number of people who are separated by a great many borders, to learn from and share with one another, is both a unique and deeply significant accomplishment.

An Ecumenical Perspective

From its very beginning BorderLinks has understood itself as a faith-based undertaking, and so anyone who desires to be part of its program is asked to be comfortable with this commitment. "Faith-based" is construed broadly, however, as BorderLinks is a truly ecumenical organization. The faith-based character of BorderLinks is not worn on its sleeve, and not all participants are Christian, but the concern to be faithful to the spirituality of the inclusive and justice-seeking message of the Scriptures is embodied in the daily lives and work of those involved. Taking its cue from the prophet Micah, BorderLinks has always tried "to seek justice, practice mercy, and walk humbly with God." [Micah 6:8] In addition there is the desire to be faithful to Jesus' statement of his own mission, "to announce good news to the poor, to proclaim release for prisoners and recovery of sight for the blind; to let the broken victims go free, to proclaim the year of the Lord's favor." [Luke 4:19]

One of the guiding lights for BorderLinks' understanding of the Judeo-Christian view of economic justice is the work of activist-theologian, Ched Myers. Myers has been extremely supportive of BorderLinks' efforts over the years, and his two-part article in *Sojourners* magazine (vol. 27, nos. 3 and 4, 1998) provides an excellent summary of the BorderLinks perspective. The articles are entitled "God Speed the Year of Jubilee" and "Jesus' New Economy of Grace," respectively. The quotation of a few passages from Myers' articles will bring into clear focus the scriptural vision behind the BorderLinks adventure. When discussing the Sabbath law, Myers says:

The social justice code of Exodus 23 extends the Sabbath cycle to a seventh year: 'You shall let the land rest and lie fallow, so that the poor of your people eat; and what they leave so the wild animals may eat.' The Sabbath year restores equilibrium by restraining the activity of 'productive' members of the economy and freeing constraints upon those who have been marginalized, both the disenfranchised, the poor, and the undomesticated, wild animals...The Deuteronomist goes even further, interpreting the Sabbath year to include debt release (Deuteronomy 15:1-18). The Sabbath year debt release intends to safeguard both social justice and sound fiscal policy, anticipating the human tendency toward selfishness, the Deuteronomist forbids people from tightening credit in the years immediately prior to the Sabbath remission.

The fullest expression of the Sabbath logic is the Levitical 'Jubilee;' a comprehensive remission to take place every 'Sabbath's Sabbath' or 49th to 50th year (Leviticus 25). The Jubilee aimed to dismantle structures of socio-economic inequality by releasing each community member from debt, returning encumbered or forfeited land to its original owners, and freeing slaves. The rationale for this unilateral restructuring of the communities' assets was to remind Israel that the land belongs to God and they are an Exodus people who must never return to a system of slavery.

Moving on to a consideration of the New Testament view, Myers has this to say:

> The most well-known appropriation of the Jubilee vision is found in Isaiah 61:1-2, the prophetic commission that begins with a call to 'bring good news to the oppressed poor' and ends with a proclamation of 'the year of the Lord's favor.' Of all the possibilities in his scripture, it is this text that Jesus of Nazareth chose to define and inaugurate his mission, according to Luke's gospel (Luke 4:18-19).

> Jesus' call for radical social restructuring at all levels from the household (Mark 3:31-35) to the body politic (Mark:10:35-45) is summarized by the Jubilee ultimatum: 'Many who are first shall be last, and the last first.' (Mark 10:31) He typically chose the venue of table fellowship in order to both show and tell object lessons that illustrate this. Meals lay at the heart of ancient society; where, what, and with whom you ate defined your social identity and status. Thus the table was a mirror of society, with its economic classes and political divisions. In the extended banquet story in Luke 14, Jesus systematically undermines prevailing conventions and proprieties, while advocating a new "table" of compassion and equality.

The above quotations explain clearly why BorderLinks is drawn to the vision of the elimination of the socioeconomic barriers and borders that separate the rich from the poor, for all of Myer's interpretation applies directly to the situation on the U.S.-Mexico border. The Incarnational Gospel of reconciliation between God and humans, and among people themselves, requires a radical rethinking of the meaning and purpose of our socio-political structures, both nationally and internationally.

John Fife, Pastor of Southside Presbyterian Church in Tucson, has not only provided a strong thread of continuity between the Sanctuary Movement and the BorderLinks' ministry, but continues to serve as a crucial source of inspiration and wisdom for all those working along the border. In an interview published in the magazine *The Other Side* (vol.33, no.1, Jan-Feb,1997) entitled "Holy Communion," Fife pinpointed the significance of the border, both as fact and as a metaphor for the future. The following quotations from this interview summarize the main themes of his perspective on the importance of "border crossing."

> The U.S.-Mexico border is the place where the issues that affect everyone in the world now come most sharply into focus. It is the only place in all the world where the Third World directly joins the First World, separated only

by a high metal wall or a cyclone fence topped with barbed wire.

But whether you are at the border or on a family farm in Iowa, in a small town in Idaho, or in a major metropolitan area on the east coast, the issues here affect you and will for the next century.

Two things are universal. One is the way the, global economy is going to determine our future; no matter where we are, we're all going to be affected by it. Second, we're all being affected by the values of the market economy, which are global as well. We are witnessing the most powerful evangelization in the world the values of the market economy are, being advocated and articulated to the whole earth.

Across the globe we face the challenge of developing institutions that will put appropriate restraints on capital; enforcing environmental integrity, safe working conditions, and appropriate wage rates for labor. We also must see that the social infrastructure exists to allow communities to provide public education, health care, and recreational facilities that build just and viable communities. The church is—and this is where the unique opportunity for the church comes in—the only global organization currently existing that is capable of taking on that task. It has an organization at the grassroots of communities throughout the world, and it has a theology and ideology that proclaim that we are brothers and sisters, that there are no boundaries of race, creed, nation, ethnic group, or any other that prevent us from being one in the Spirit.

We also face the challenge of articulating a different value system that will provide people with choices and elevate people out of the death-dealing aspects of the market economy and into a new kind of community with a different set of allegiances altogether.

We're going to have to develop global treaties on the treatment of labor and the ability of labor to organize.

We're going to have to develop institutions like the United Nations that can bring together the many involved groups. We're going to have to develop a global environmental system of regulations so that rogue corporations can't go across the Mexican border and start dumping toxic wastes and materials into the air, water, and earth. And we're going to have to develop a set of agreements between nations and communities that will provide a just and viable society through public schools and health institutions.

There are opportunities for churches all across the country to come to the border, to experience the issues, and to educate people on those issues. But beyond that, every congregation should establish connections with a church somewhere else in the world.

Our brothers and sisters in the Faith are the poor and oppressed and suffering people of the world, folks who are living in places where Christ is being crucified. We have to make a fundamental choice: we can either be in community with them, or we choose to remain isolated in the U.S. empire. We North Americans still see ourselves as the center of Christendom and as bearers of the Gospel. That's absolute nonsense in today's world. Christians in North America and western Europe need to understand that the center of Christendom is no longer here. It is moving south as fast as the Spirit can move.

The reality is that BorderLinks is continually having to work against conditions that are largely the result of United States policies. Not only was the border originally created as a result of the U.S. invasion of Mexico, but its ongoing history has always been one of conflict and exploitation. The barriers installed by the United States' pattern of behavior toward its Mexican neighbors are not only political and economic, but are racial and religious as well. Now the United States government has erected a physical wall between our two countries that powerfully symbolizes U.S. fear and disdain of the Mexican people. BorderLinks works to dismantle this wall.

Conclusion

The Search for Humane Borders

The examples of Bishop Samuel Ruíz and the organization BorderLinks as described in the last two chapters of this book allow us to visualize very real ways in which Christians and others are living out a Borderland Theology today. Being able to see, hear, and touch these examples gives hope to the doubter within us. We begin to believe that the ideal of greater justice and inclusion in this world is not an unreachable utopia or the foolish pursuit of dreamers. If God calls us to cross borders and break down barriers, it is not a call to a vague or impossible mission. A faithful life in the borderlands is within our reach, and if we should choose such a life, we will not be alone!

Fortunately, there are also many other cases of inspiring border-crossing witness in our world. In Latin America, amid many material difficulties, examples abound. Just south of Mexico, for instance, in the Diocese of San Marcos, Guatemala, Bishop Alvaro Ramazzini has risked his comfort, his privilege, and even his life to defend the poor of his area. He has been an active supporter of truth and reconciliation for human rights victims and has worked tirelessly to attain land rights for peasant farmers. As the coffee crisis and declining economy force large-scale migration from his Diocese, he has developed a sister relationship with the Diocese of Wilmington, Delaware, which is located in an area where many of his parishioners now labor in poultry packing plants. In Guatemala he has opened a hospitality center for immigrants deported from Mexico and the United States.

In another kind of example, 600 some *mestizo* and indigenous lay leaders of the Catholic Church crossed formidable boundaries of fear and mistrust to collect more than 8,000 testimonies from civilian victims of Guatemala's 36-year civil war. The inter-Diocesan project, which complemented the postwar United Nations Historical Clarification Commission (or "truth commission") Report, is called the Recovery of Historic Memory (REMHI) project. As one lay leader, Rodolfo Godines, said, "Our community was crushed into pieces like a clay pot. Through the REMHI project, I sat with people in their homes, and we cried together as they told about what they had suffered during the war. With the telling of these painful but sacred stories, we are putting the pieces back together again." Bishop Juan Gerardi, the founder of the REMHI project, was assassinated in 1998 but the work continues in the efforts of courageous lay people like Rodolfo Godines.

In the United States, there are also endless opportunities for serving in the borderlands. While the borders in question do not have to be geographical borders, these national boundaries do provide especially fertile ground for borderland reflection and witness in the 21st century. My own experience in Arizona leads me to focus on the U.S.-Mexico border and so I would like to close with another snapshot of this border area which is in need of so much attention both in terms of just policy and urgent humanitarian needs.

The U.S.-Mexico Border

The U.S.-Mexico border was set up at the conclusion of the Mexican-American war in 1848. Initially it followed the Gila and Rio Grande Rivers, but in 1854 it was moved about 100 miles south in Arizona, as a result of the Gadsden Purchase so that the United States could build the Union Pacific railroad through to California. A great many Mexican, as well as Chinese, workers were imported to provide the manual labor for this project. In the years between 1854 and the end of World War II, both Mexican and American citizens moved back and forth across the border rather freely. Mexican family members who had been separated by the arbitrary border, as well as shoppers and tourists, had little difficulty crossing back and forth.

From time to time during this period, whenever it served its economic purposes, the U.S. government developed special programs, such as the Braceros Plan, to sponsor temporary Mexican workers. In recent decades, however, the United States has steadily increased its militarization of the border in part to inhibit the flow of illegal drugs, but also to make it more difficult for undocumented immigrants to cross the border. In the early 1990s a 12-foot steel wall was erected in each of the major border cities to supplement the many miles of barbed-wire fences across the rural and desert areas of the

Conclusion: The Search for Humane Borders   113

border. Within the past few years the U.S. government has greatly increased the budget and manpower, as well as the surveillance technology, all along the border. Millions of dollars have been spent for more powerful military equipment and thousands of new Border patrol agents have been placed on what is called Operation Gatekeeper. Mexican citizens can no longer cross easily into the United States since it is difficult and expensive to obtain passports and visas for shopping and family visitation.

Part of the rationale for this greatly increased border control pertains to the introduction in 1994 of the North American Free Trade Agreement (NAFTA), which allows goods and profits to flow freely across the border, but prohibits Mexican workers from doing so. Border security has also been greatly intensified since the terrorist attacks of September 11, 2001. Under the current logic, both drugs and terrorists must be kept out; so Mexican workers must be as well. A major result of this crackdown on the border is that the thousands of Mexican and Central American migrants seeking work in the United States now focus their border crossing efforts on the vast desert regions, far from the cities and main Border Patrol stations.

The tragedy is that in so doing they greatly increase their risk of dying, especially in the summer months, of heat exhaustion. Every year between 75 and 150 migrants die in the desert, and many more are rescued just short of death. As the Immigration and Naturalization Service (INS) has now been subsumed under the Department of Homeland Security, we can expect more of these deaths. Fear of terrorism will lead to more drastic measures to stop undocumented immigrants, and immigrants will be forced to take even riskier measures to come to the United States.

The great irony of this current border situation is that not only do Mexican and other migrants desperately need work, but those that do manage to get across the border almost always find work immediately. The simple fact is that our economy needs these workers as much as they need the work. There are probably at least 3 million undocumented Mexican laborers in the United States. Not only do these workers pay their Social Security taxes, but the vast majority never stay in the United States more than a few years and thus never collect their benefits. To top it off, these workers work at jobs that the majority of U.S.-American citizens would be unwilling to accept.

Why do they keep coming? They come because the best paying jobs in Mexico, in the *maquiladora* industry along the entire border, pay about $1 an hour, one-tenth of what can be earned on the U.S. side of the border. These assembly plant jobs are all that is left for the Mexican labor force now that agribusiness interests have taken over nearly all of the farmland in order to produce crops for export rather than for domestic consumption.

Here is how Jack McGarvey, an Arizona writer who lives near the border, describes the situation of his friend Arturo who lives across the border with his family in Nogales, Sonora:

> When his son needs a pair of shoes, Arturo must spend an entire week's salary. When Arturo buys beans and rice to nurture his family, they cost him 20 percent more than what I pay on this side of the border. Arturo spends at least 70 percent of his income for food to feed his family of three—not much leftover for a pair of shoes.... They live in a flimsy cardboard and tin-roofed house which has a single electric line strung up from a new line from an adjoining street. They have just enough to power two light bulbs. Arturo and Ruth have no piped-in fresh water and must buy five gallon jugs from a vendor. They spend 10 percent of Arturo's weekly income to drink fresh water.... Sometimes Arturo is tempted to cross the border.... If he should, who among us Americans could feign surprise? ("Why They Come?" *Arizona Daily Star*, June 16, 2002.)

Hospitality on the Border

Into the midst of this socio-political and economic quagmire a faith-based organization called Humane Borders has intervened. The main force behind this coalition of individuals and groups, BorderLinks included, is Robin Hoover, the pastor of the First Christian Church in Tucson. The stated goal of Humane Borders is to provide water stations across the vast desert regions of the Arizona-Mexico border to help alleviate the suffering and death experienced by so many migrants seeking work in the United States. Hoover sums up Humane Borders' efforts in these words: "We must take death out of the migration equation...Part of our mission is to tell this story...We favor policy changes that will get people out of the desert." (*Tucson Weekly*, June 13, 2002)

Here, then, is a group of people living and working on the U.S.-Mexico border, striving to actually cross the borders created by the U.S. border policy. These faithful volunteers place large containers of water, along with a blue flag on a plastic pole, along the most frequently followed paths of migrants making their way across the desert. Surprisingly enough, the Border Patrol has been, by and large, basically cooperative with these humanitarian efforts.

In the desert a cup of cold water serves as both a literal gift and as a symbol of giving. One cannot help be reminded in this context of Jesus' teaching about sharing a drink of cold water in Matthew 25: "In as much as you did it unto them, you did it unto me." But some local ranchers and farmers have the opposite reaction to the many migrants making their way across the border. They claim that not only do migrants take jobs away from U.S.-American workers, but that they sometimes trash property, steal, cut fences etc. Occasionally a land owner will shoot at these trespassers in order to scare them off. Some have even formed vigilante groups.

And yet not all border dwellers succumb to the temptation of violence and hostility as they feel their territories invaded. The example of the Tohono O'odham Indian nation is an inspiring one. The reservation of these Native Americans is located along the Arizona border, and the Tohono O'odham nation has had its share of tension with migrants crossing through its territory. Their property and livestock have been damaged, and the influx of sick migrants have overtaxed their clinics and hospitals. When Humane Borders tried to negotiate the placement of water bottles on Tohono O'odham lands, there was difficulty at first as the Native Americans feared that this practice would simply draw more and more migrants across the reservation.

Eventually, however, it became clear to all involved that the real source of the problem was neither migration nor water bottles, but the U.S. government border policy. The vice chairman of the Tohono O'odham people expressed the new, united position on the border situation in these words: "The issue now is to end this policy of death. We condemn the policy known as Operation Gatekeeper because it is a policy of death. We will not stand by silently as our neighbors die.... The sands of our sacred desert are forever stained with the blood of our neighbors, our brothers and sisters, our sons and daughters—in the eyes of our Great Creator we are one."

Mike Wilson, a Native American and pastor of the local Presbyterian Church at the time, reinforced this position with these words: "The death, the pain, the suffering, the torture must stop now. Our neighbors are not criminals; they only come north to feed their families. You and I would do the same for our children. For this they do not deserve the death penalty [both quotations from the *Arizona Daily Star*, June 18, 2002].

As the debate has continued the position has changed somewhat. Some of the members of the Tohono O'odham Nation now take the position that while it is right to allow the migrating Latin Americans to come across the border onto and through their reservation, they do not want the Human Borders volunteers to place water containers in the desert on the Reservation. Local opinion, even among the Humane Borders volunteers, is divided on how to resolve this issue.

The most recent development in this search for a way to make the border more humane is the introduction of what is called the "Samaritan Patrol." A number of the people involved in the Humane Borders operation were concerned that simply placing water stations in the desert in the hopes that migrants would find them was not enough. The Samaritan Patrol now involves volunteers who patrol the border area in four-wheel drive vehicles in hopes of encountering migrants before they actually run into problems in order to offer them food, water, and first aid. The difficulty here is how to define their task so that they are able to be of assistance without breaking the law. As United States immigration law now stands, helping someone without the proper documents to cross the border is a crime. The volunteers are trained in first-aid and receive instructions concerning how much and what sort of help they can provide the people they encounter. It remains to be seen how effective this effort will turn out to be, though so far, it has been quite successful.

Humane Borders has received a good deal of attention from the national news media and this is indeed part of its stated goal, namely to call attention to the plight of the immigrants in order to get our national border policy changed. While no one has an easy formula for a perfect immigration policy, there are several steps that could be taken to begin to take down the hostile walls at the U.S.-Mexico border. Many people have long advocated a temporary work permit or visa for Mexican laborers one that would allow them to work in the United States legally. This would not only greatly reduce the number of deaths in the desert, but would be good for our own economy as well.

After all, very few U.S. citizens are willing to lay asphalt or pick lettuce for a living. U.S. employers are constantly looking for people to work in minimum wage jobs, but U.S. policy makes it difficult for Mexican immigrants to come and take them. Not surprisingly, of course, workers still come. But they come without documents, accept work below minimum wage, and are afraid to speak out against mistreatment and abuse. U.S. corporations have their cheap labor force either way, but which way is more humane?

Once allowances are made for Mexican labor, of course, there must be allowances for those who are desperate to feed their families in Guatemala, El Salvador and the rest of Central and South America. This is where many United States citizens start drawing lines. Fear can overtake us and we imagine ourselves being engulfed in a tide of angry, poor people from the South. We may deny it to ourselves, but often we may find ourselves building walls in our hearts to protect our privileges.

But the truth is that not everyone wants to come to the United States. What people want and need is to make a living and provide a dignified life for their families. For this reason, a just and rational immigration policy must begin with a just global economic policy, one that allows Central American and Mexican farmers to survive on their own lands, one that provides jobs that can support families everywhere, not just in the United States. We cannot allow ourselves to be so paralyzed by fear that we are unable to see the root causes of human need. When we open our hearts to visit the borderlands of our world, we realize that we are all connected. We cannot enrich ourselves at the expense of others. We are all in this together.

To me it is clear that those who participate in BorderLinks, Humane Borders, and the Samaritan Patrol are people with a highly developed commitment to a Borderland Theology. They embody the Gospel of God's love and grace, and are willing to assume the risks that this demands. Just as God's Incarnation in Jesus required a "border crossing" from the divine to the human, so these different reincarnations of that same sacrificial love require various degrees and styles of border crossing. People who find ways to promote love and justice in the borderlands make real the all-inclusive grace of God.

The Gospel and the Borderlands

A Borderland Theology understanding of the Christian Gospel is extremely profound and at the same time abstract. However, when one learns about and interacts with the specific people and ministries engaged in faithful borderland living, the understanding become far more concrete and direct. A Borderland Theology can be and is being lived by real people.

World history and current events show that power relations between peoples have always been defined by borders. From Genghis Khan and the Toltec Empire, through Greco-Roman and Medieval times, right up to the present conflicts in Ireland, Yugoslavia, Palestine, Africa, and Afghanistan, the central issues have always been, "Who was here first?" and "Who gets to draw the line where?" It is my belief that unless and until we can learn to overcome the desire to erect exclusionary and oppressive boundaries between peoples, we shall never have anything like world peace. The Gospel of God's love and grace has much to offer in the reflection of such global issues.

Finally, I believe the notion of "border" serves as a metaphor for other areas and dimensions of life. Everyday human life, on both the personal and social level, is made up of many borders and barriers that divide people from one another. The sorts of estrangement and alienation that we all confront on a daily basis are as much in need of crossing and overcoming as are those political borders that

Conclusion: The Search for Humane Borders

have been the focus of this entire book. People seeking to be true to the Incarnational Gospel will find ways to dissolve and diminish these psycho-socio borders as well. Our families, our neighborhoods, our churches, our places of work, and the political domains within which we all live stand in need of being infused with the love and grace of God as revealed in the inclusive, border-crossing, justice-seeking example of Jesus Christ.

Appendices

Questions for Reflection

In a Borderland Theology, believers are called to cross or dissolve the barriers that exclude, oppress, and separate people from each other. To understand this call fully, we must dwell for a time in the borderlands.

1. Where are the borderlands of our own lives and communities? (Where are people separated from each other? Where do the boundaries between privileged insiders and marginalized outsiders exist in our communities and daily lives? Are they interpersonal, religious, social, economic, geographic, or political boundaries?)

2. How can we better understand these borderlands? How can we dwell in them? Are we prepared to enter the borderlands with humility, knowing that we must listen and learn *before* we act and *as* we act?

3. In what ways does the "Word become flesh" when people choose to live their faith in these borderlands?

4. How and in which direction is God already crossing the borders around us? Are the marginalized teaching the privileged? Are the privileged reaching out to the marginalized with repentance and renewed commitment?

5. What risks do we take when we enter the borderlands of our communities? What do we need to strengthen us to help us to take these risks?

6. If we only reflect, we have not crossed borders. If we only act, we may not cross borders with the humility, knowledge, and integrity that is called for. How can we make sure that we are continually moving in a cycle of both action and reflection?

Resource Organizations

American Friends Service Committee
1129 G Street
San Diego, CA 92101
(619) 233-4114
www.afsc.org/immigrants-rights/
AFSC is a Quaker group with links to projects, documents, and resources addressing the U.S.-Mexico border, including their detailed border abuse reports.

Border Environmental Justice Campaign
1717 Kettner Blvd., Suite 100
San Diego, CA 92101
(619) 235-0281
www.environmentalhealth.org/border.html
This campaign highlights the health risks facing residents and workers in the San Diego/Tijuana border region due to industrial contamination. Information on maquiladoras and free trade.

BorderLinks
1040 N First Avenue
Tucson AZ 85719
520-628-8263
www.borderlinks.org
Borderlinks conducts travel seminars focusing on the issues of Mexican border communities where people from the north and south explore global issues in the stark reality of the border environment.

Maquiladora Health & Safety Support Network
P.O. Box 124
Berkeley, CA 9470
(510) 558-1014
www.mhssn.igc.org
This network provides information regarding workplace hazards in maquiladoras along the U.S.-Mexico border, as well as information about health and safety complaints filed under NAFTA.

Religious Taskforce on Central America and Mexico
3053 Fourth St. NE
Washington, DC 20017
202-529-0441
www.rtfcam.org
A resource for education, action and faith reflection on Central America and Mexico.

Witness for Peace
1229 15th St. NW
Washington, D.C. 20005
202-588-1471
www.witnessforpeace.org
Education and action for human rights, peace, justice and sustainable development in the hemisphere.

Migrant Deaths in 2002

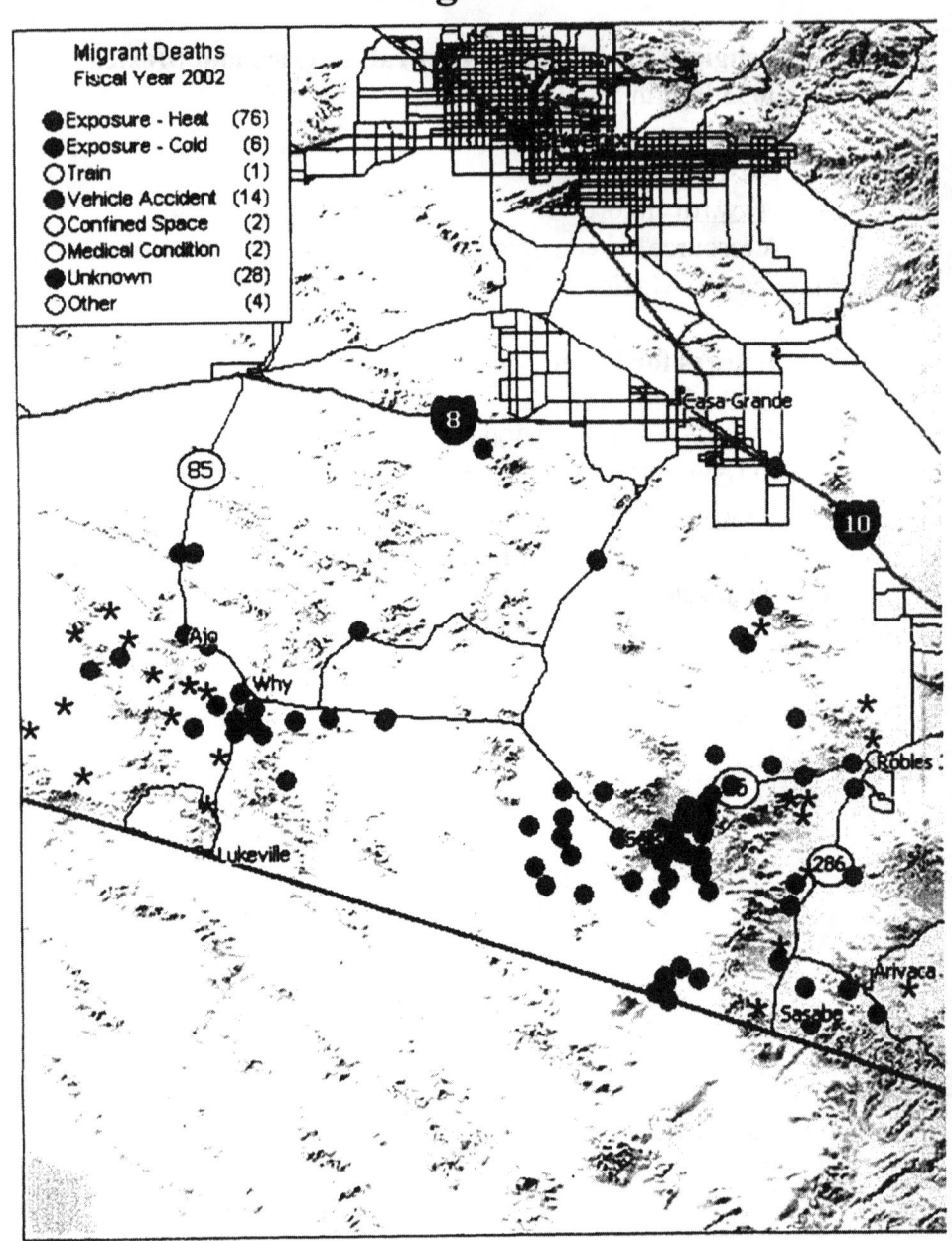

Along the Arizona-Mexico Border

About the Author

Jerry Gill is the Academic Coordinator for BorderLinks in Tucson, Arizona. He has degrees from Westmont College, the University of Washington, New York Theological Seminary, and Duke University, and has taught philosophy and religious studies at small liberal arts colleges around the country for over 40 years.

He has authored some 25 books including *Native American Worldviews* (Humanity Books, 2002) and over 100 journal articles. Jerry plays basketball and sculpts for hobbies, and loves to travel. He is married to Mari Sorri, who hails from Finland and works as a professional clay artist. She also is the House Manager for BorderLinks.

www.ingramcontent.com/pod-product-compliance
Lightning Source LLC
Chambersburg PA
CBHW070919160426
43193CB00011B/1521